THE THINGS
OF THE WORLD

THE THINGS
OF THE WORLD
A Social Phenomenology

James A. Aho

PRAEGER

Westport, Connecticut
London

301
A28t

Library of Congress Cataloging-in-Publication Data

Aho, James Alfred, 1942–
    The things of the world : a social phenomenology / James A. Aho.
    p. cm.
    Includes bibliographical references (p.   ) and index.
    ISBN 0–275–96247–4 (alk. paper).—ISBN 0–275–96248–2 (pbk. :
alk. paper)
    1. Phenomenological sociology. 2. Sociology—Philosophy.
3. Self. I. Title.
    HM24.A453 1998
    301—dc21   98–23566

British Library Cataloguing in Publication Data is available.

Library of Congress Catalog Card Number: 98–23566
ISBN: 0–275–96247–4
        0–275–96248–2 (pbk.)

First published in 1998

Praeger Publishers, 88 Post Road West, Westport, CT 06881
An imprint of Greenwood Publishing Group, Inc.

Printed in the United States of America

The paper used in this book complies with the
Permanent Paper Standard issued by the National
Information Standards Organization (Z39.48–1984).

10 9 8 7 6 5 4 3 2 1

Copyright Acknowledgments

The author and publisher gratefully acknowledge permission for use of the following material:

Excerpts from "The Apocalypse of Modernity" by James Aho, in *Millennium,
Messiahs, and Mayhem: Contemporary Apocalyptic Movements*, ed. Thomas Rob-
bins and Susan Palmer (New York: Routledge, 1997).

Excerpts from "A Phenomenology of the Enemy" in *This Thing of Darkness: A
Sociology of the Enemy* by James Aho (Seattle: University of Washington Press,
1994).

Excerpts from "The Recent Ethnogenesis of 'White Man' " by James Aho. *Left
Bank 5* (December 1993): 55–64.

*If anyone says that the one true God, . . . cannot be
known with certainty by the natural light of human
reason, by means of the things that are made, let
him be anathema.*

Pope Pius X, *On Modernity*

Contents

Acknowledgments

As always, my colleagues at Idaho State University have provided the wherewithall to complete this book. The first draft of *The Things of the World* was written while on sabbatical in 1995. Without the uninterrupted time and financial support of this academic sabbath, the book's completion would have been inconceivable. I also want to thank Michael Blain, Boise State University, for reading, critiquing, and affirming an earlier version of the manuscript.

The Things of the World emerged from a regular class offering, "Mind, Self and Society," the title of which was stolen directly from George Herbert Mead. I still recall the chill of excitement when I stumbled across Mead's lectures as an undergraduate years ago. I am grateful for the indulgence of my own students upon whom the ideas in this book were first inflicted.

I am indebted to my immediate family—my wife Margaret, and adult sons Ken, Kevin, and Kyle. Each, by bringing beautiful things into being in the form of art, music, poetry, and the athlete's dance, remain a constant source of inspiration. This is to say nothing of their having "walked the walk," and of thus serving as fountains of emotional support whenever my own creative waters have threatened to run dry.

I have profited particularly from hours-long conversations with Kevin, more than once in idyllic mountain settings. In his enthusiastic response to phenomenology, he lent plausibility to a new way of thinking and seeing the things closest to me.

1

INTRODUCTION

This book concerns the things of the world: me, you, we, them, and "it." With respect to me, the book deals first of all with my "mind-stuff," the way I see things, think about them, remember them. Of course, the most beguiling object in my line of sight, the object of my most avid ruminations, the preoccupation of my recollections, is my very own self. What is "self" in its various guises—identity, esteem, and image? Why are they *as* they are?

Regarding you, I am interested in what appears to be a simple question, "How do I know you?" I take it for granted that knowing you is unproblematic and natural; rarely do I inquire into the basis for this blithe confidence. Is my knowledge of you rational and objective? Or does it rest on *feelings* of mutuality?

Besides having a mind, I am endowed with flesh. I emote, enjoy things, suffer. Some of my pains are due to illness. What exactly is an illness? How do illnesses arise? Furthermore, why in treating the misfortunes of sickness do we often resort to administering more pain? Concerning pleasure, if it is truly the satisfaction of desire, then how do desires come to be? In particular, why have the limitless possibilities of pleasure been channeled into sexuality? For what reason do we have these obsessions with homosexuality and addiction?

I share the world with others. Some of these are objects of vilification—enemies. With some—communities—I feel a certain one-ness because they have the same skin color, yearnings, maladies, language, or faith as myself. There are also others I neither hate nor identify with, but must attend to in order to accomplish my goals—associations. I not only experience each of these others differently, but also look at myself differently in the presence of each. Why is this so? How does each type of other come to be what it is for me?

Finally, there is a procession to the things of the world. One thing always follows another. Things are always "in time." What is time? How does time become the thing it is for me?

In the 1980s in Boise, Idaho, I attended a lecture by Ray Cuzzort, then of the University of Colorado. It was a professional conference and the audience had long since been narcoticized by the morning's droning voices, when Cuzzort arose to tell us that now that sociology had been fully assimilated into the modern university, it no longer needed to pretend it was a science like chemistry or physics. Stop the masquerade of ethical neutrality, he admonished us, take off the lab coats, put an end to contrived experiments and petty surveys. The time has come to confess to what we have been up to all along, namely, telling stories.

Sociology is storytelling, Cuzzort said, and any bard worth his or her muster is armed with a passel of tales to interpret any event. There are the functionalist line, the Marxist account, the interactionist spin, the cultural viewpoint, a liberal-individualist narrative, and so forth. The difference between good sociology and poor sociology, he continued, is not that the first more closely approximates objective truth. Instead, it is that it grabs the audience's attention because it is a tale artfully, engagingly, told. A good story has boldly drawn characters: villains, heroes, victims, fools. It resonates with suspense, mystery, irony, and paradox. It relates the tragedy of boundless aspirations coming up against human limits. In other words and above all, good sociology promotes self-recognition. The reader and listener see themselves in a tale well told. They "re-know" themselves, and in so doing come to possess consciously what they already were, but were not fully aware of. This book takes Cuzzort's recommendation to heart. I will count it successful if it occasions in readers the "aha" of having been reintroduced to things already dimly familiar, themselves and their world.

PHENOMENOLOGY CHARACTERIZED

How are the things of the world ordinarily experienced? How are they thought, felt, recalled, and seen by the average person? I call the experiential realm "phenomena." The systematic study of phenomena is phenomenology.[1] This book is a student's and layperson's introduction to social phenomenology. I emphasize *social* in part to indicate that although I may occasionally allude to the ethical, epistemological, and ontological issues raised by phenomenology, I do not intend to address them in any complete way. These are matters for philosophy, and would take me into waters far beyond my accustomed depth. The concern of this book is solely with the things standing right here, period. This also means that I will not be dealing with "phenomena" in the popular sense of the word, that is, with esoteric, paranormal events, mystical visions, and the like. While these fall within the domain of social phenomenology, this book focuses primarily on the quotidian, or what Peter Berger has called "paramount reality," everyday things: me, you, them, we, and it; the body's moods and desires; its afflictions and pleasures; the passage of these through time. Following well-established precedent, I call these objects the elements of the life- or lived-world (*Lebenswelt*).[2] My intention is to deal with the life-world in three ways.

Descriptive Phenomenology

First, each of the entities enumerated above is phenomenologically described. The goal in each case is to "reduce" reports of personal experiences and other primary documents to the presumed prototypical or average experience of the thing in question, its "ideal-essence," those elements of the experience without which it could not be.[3] Take, for example, the phenomenon of dying. For years thanatologists have gathered reports about near-death episodes from a variety of drastically compromised accident victims, wounded soldiers, and terminally ill patients to construct the ideal-typical death experience. Presumably, it involves moving through a dark tunnel toward a light source, being received by deceased relatives, and being engulfed by a feeling likened to "love."[4]

The point to emphasize in this example is not its evident accuracy (or lack thereof). It is, instead, to note that like the products of any inquiry, social phenomenological claims are based on "data"—in the example above, on reports of near-death events. This is why it might be said that although it deals with personal experiences, phenomenology may still be considered a "rigorous" enterprise.[5]

Genetic Phenomenology

My second task is to sociologically account for how the various entities of the life-world have been "accomplished," that is, how the prototypical experiences of the things in question have come to be.[6] For instance, I examine how human beings are routinely transmogrified into excremental icons (enemies) fit for "elimination"; how that widely disparaged object known as "white man" came into existence; how pain is "socially produced"; how heterosexuality and drug addiction have been "manufactured" by self-interested well-doers. It is at this point that I turn away from Edmund Husserl of the *Cartesian Meditations*, the considered founder of modern phenomenology.

According to Husserl, all the world's things are constituted, they come to stand before me as the things they are, by means of the "irreducible features" of what he calls the "transcendent Ego." "The objective world, the world that exists for me, that always has and always will exist for me, the only world that ever can exist for me—this world, with all its objects . . . derives its whole sense and its existential status . . . from me myself, *from me as the transcendent Ego*."[7]

This book rejects the Husserlian thesis. My position is that the allegedly irreducible Ego, the so-called universal and timeless Author of all things, is *itself* a social-cultural product. Ego is but one aspect of the life-world, specifically, the world of modernity. Hence, it can hardly be considered its ultimate Source. A more detailed account of ego is provided later. Here, it is enough to say that ego (as an autonomous, free-willed, precious being) emerges historically out of a milieu of heroic sagas, religious discourse, civil court proceedings, and commerce.

What this all boils down to is this: If ego is indeed a product of social-historical circumstances, then the same must also be true for those things presumably issuing from it. Just what might these circumstances be? In this book they are all encompassed under the word "conversation." *The things of the world arise from conversation.* So said, Husserl's theory can be rephrased thus: The objective world, the world that exists for me, the only world that can exist for me, derives its sense and being *from us together as conversants*: from oral and written communications, both extemporaneous and routinized, verbal and physical (as in "body talk"), private and public.

As will be seen later, conversation accomplishes the world in either of two ways: First, it *transforms* stuff into what was "never there before," turning it into marriages, property rights, currencies, authorities, and so forth. Second, it *discloses* (aspects of) things "already there" in-themselves, like rocks, dogs, or water.[8]

Of course, it should be kept in mind that while we use conversation to frame the things of the world, the medium of conversation, language, also "uses" us. We not only create the world with words, words "re-create" us after their own logic and parameters. While in this book I emphasize the fabrication of worlds by people, enough pauses will be taken to remind the reader that the opposite is also true: as we absorb a language, the world sustained by it "reabsorbs" us, making us its own.

Lest I be accused of substituting a form of social-centrism for egocentrism, the following comments should suffice. Throughout this book, even if not explicitly stated, I assume a distinction between Earth and the life-world, or as Martin Heidegger, a student of Husserl's might have said, between Being and "being-there" (*Dasein*). *Being* is the presuppositional possibility for our being-in-the-world at a particular time and place, surrounded by a corpus of things. *Being-there* refers to our spatial/temporal immersion in that very corpus. It is our existence amidst a coherency of material, ideal, and social things, each with its own characteristics. Being, to express it differently, is the Gift that makes the world possible.[9] The life-world is what, by talking, we make of the Gift. Through the things we build by discourse, the Gift is revealed.

Destructive Phenomenology

Third, to describe how the things of the world are socially constituted, whether by invention or by disclosure, is in effect to destabilize it. To use Heidegger's harsher terms, it is to "destroy" or "destructure" the world.[10] For if the world is shown to be our joint project, then it need not be as it appears.

To the average person the life-world is experienced in what Husserl calls the naive or "natural attitude."[11] This means that the world's things present themselves to consciousness as being parts of an understandable coherency; that they are taken as given in the nature of things-themselves, and hence not essentially alterable; that they therefore *must* be, should be, have to be what they are; and that insofar as this is the case, then all reasonably sane persons must perceive them the same way.

Phenomenology adopts an artfully diplomatic stance toward this attitude. To begin with, it considers the natural attitude to be the way eminently rational people ordinarily are in the world, if they are to survive and flourish. Society would simply disintegrate were its members continually questioning its reality, its necessity, and its enduringness, were they to distrust everything, including their own and other people's substantiality. It hardly needs to be said that phenomenologists themselves assume the natural attitude when they remove their analytic spectacles and step into the everydayness of raising children, going to work, or running for office.

On the other hand, phenomenology also insists that the natural attitude is a false, "alienated," way of being in the world.[12] For while the life-world *seems* to have an ontology independent of our consciousness of it, in truth it is produced and sustained by "ceaseless reality work."[13] That is, the things of the world are what they are for us as a result of conversation in the sense described above. Like any human creation, then, these things are fragile; they need not be to others what they are for me. When done well, phenomenological destruction shatters the trancelike hold of the natural attitude. I am momentarily liberated from the sway of worldly things.

Take lived-time, an event so intimate as to hardly deserve a second thought. It was the American ethnographer Benjamin Whorf who first described how thoroughly different temporal order is for Europeans than for the Hopi, a pueblo folk residing in the Amer ican Southwest.[14] To Europeans, says Whorf, time gives itself to consciousness as an unwinding scroll on which everything can be placed either in past, present, or future. To the Hopi, on the other hand, time is simply the appearance of one thing after another. Although both lived-times are partly constituted by, and reflected in, the respective grammars of the Europeans and Hopis, neither people is aware of this. Instead, both typically experience time, along with everything else, in the natural attitude as given in the nature of things-themselves, as something that can be adjusted to, but never changed.

Whorf goes on to describe how Europeans expend considerable resources trying to position events on their cosmic time-line, conducting histories, paleontologies, and archaeologies. They use evermore precise chronometers to locate themselves on the time-scroll; they invent devices to "save" time by accelerating their passage through space. They speak of time as "money." As with other material things, they believe that time can be "killed," "wasted," "bought," and "stolen."

The prototypical Hopi adaptation to time, in contrast, revolves around "preparing," helping sun, rain, and plant life to become manifest. Preparations include public announcements by the Crier Chief of the hoped-for event; cultivation of "inner readiness" for its appearance by meditation and prayer; rehearsal for its imminent arrival through races, cooking, dancing, and smoking; and finally, "encouraging." As a European audience might do at a football game, urging the local team on, or a golfer might use his body to compel a putt into the cup, so the Hopi transmit their collective energy toward the yearned for, but yet to be.

Whenever Europeans synchronize their watches, positioning themselves precisely at the same point in lived-time, say 4:35 PM, says Whorf, their shared conviction that time indeed has spatial extension is reconfirmed. Similarly, when at dawn the sun breaks above the horizon, the Hopi breathe a sigh of relief. The efficacy of their preparations, along with their notion of time, is validated once again.

CONCLUSION

In Harold Garfinkel's so-called breaching experiments, researchers intentionally disrupt taken-for-granted activities like sidewalk greetings and restaurant encounters to learn the "methods" by which participants re-create a sense of order. The student comes to appreciate how fragile the world really is, and how hard we labor to sustain it. This may be considered an example of phenomenological destruction.[15] Another "destructive" practice, one followed here, is to affix "lived-" or "life-" before entities, as in the phrases "lived-time," "lived-body," "life-world." This reminds the reader that there is no separation between the things of the world and his or her experience of them. Still another procedure to be employed later is known as "bracketing."[16] This involves two steps: one, placing quotations around thing-words, so that they are understood *as* words; two, determining the conversational context out of which the word-things first emerged, became popularized, and are now maintained.

Why weaken the power that things ordinarily wield? Why "destroy" the world? Certainly, if the object is merely to scandalize ordinary sensibilities by displaying the ultimate meaninglessness, relativity, and artificiality of everything, then phenomenological destruction has little to recommend it. However, it may be of inestimable value if it makes us less vulnerable to elites attempting to mobilize support for their parochial interests by manipulating esteemed or defamatory social objects.[17] If it can be shown, for example, that whether they are Jews, Iraqis, gays, Communists, or "Japs," all enemies have the same ideal-essence, and that these attributed qualities are a product of collective projection, then maybe our enthusiasm for liquidating and "cleansing" them might be somewhat abated. Again, if it can be demonstrated that desires and pains, far from being merely neurological functions, are partly conversational constructs, then we may be reluctant to continue investing untold treasure and human lives to fight some of them (or preserve others).

Precisely because it undermines conventional idols, phenomenology often finds itself accused of imperiling the possibility of morality altogether. Indeed, this criticism seems to be on the mark if by moral existence is meant obedience to allegedly universal, natural rules of conduct. However, I suppose a different understanding of morality: morality as the habit of taking responsibility for all the things of the world, including those very rules. When seen from this perspective, far from crippling moral capacity, phe-

nomenology deepens and enriches it. It teaches that I am unavoid-
ably and intimately involved in the joint making and daily sus-
tenance of the world.

True, as a "destructive" enterprise phenomenology imperils the
things of the world. Just as when I fall ill, the health I earlier took
for granted assumes added value, as does the parent to the child
when the parent dies, in being (phenomenologically) endangered,
the preciousness of the world's things is revealed. Prior to their
destruction, they were "too close to be seen"; now that they are
"lost," I find them. I reappropriate them. I possess them in a new
way, a conscious way. They become truly my own for the first
time.

NOTES

1. Edmund Husserl, *Cartesian Meditations: An Introduction to Phe-
nomenology*, trans. Dorian Cairns (The Hague: Martinus Nijhoff, 1977).
Social phenomenology was imported to America in the person of Alfred
Schutz. See the latter's *Collected Papers*, vol. 1, ed. and intro. Maurice
Natanson (The Hague: Martinus Nijhoff, 1973). For a clear, yet sophis-
ticated review of Schutz, see Peter Berger and Thomas Luckmann, *The
Social Construction of Reality* (Garden City, NY: Doubleday-Anchor,
1967).

2. The phenomenological concept of life-world was coined by Edmund Husserl, "Philosophy and the Crisis of European Man," in his *Phenomenology and the Crisis of Philosophy* (New York: Harper and Row,
1965), p. 150. The sense in which it is used here, however, is indebted to
Alfred Schutz and Thomas Luckmann, *The Structures of the Life-World*,
trans. Richard Zaner and H. Tristam Engelhardt Jr. (Evanston, IL: Northwestern University Press, 1973), pp. 3–6.

3. For Husserl, "ideal essence" (*eidos*) means the features of the
knower (the "transcendent Ego") that make the experience of a thing possible (*Cartesian Meditations*, pp. 69–72). As used here, it refers only to
the ideal-typical features of the experience itself.

4. I. Stevenson and B. Greyson, "The Phenomenology of Near-Death
Experiences," *American Journal of Psychiatry* 137 (1980): 1193–95. See
also E. A. Maitz and R. J. Pekala, "Phenomenological Quantification of
an Out-of-Body Experience Associated with a Near-Death Event," *Omega*
22 (1990/91): 199–214.

5. Husserl considers phenomenology "rigorous" because it presumably provides an ultimate ground from which philosophy can begin,

namely, the indubitable features of the transcendent ego (*Cartesian Meditations*, pp. 11–14). It should be clear that I am using the word "rigorous" merely to emphasize that social phenomenology is analogous to any other social inquiry. I am not saying that my claims correspond to some fundamental "truth," objective or otherwise.

6. Occasionally, Husserl calls this "genetic phenomenology" to distinguish it from "descriptive phenomenology" (Husserl, *Cartesian Meditations*), pp. 75f.

7. Ibid., p. 26. Husserl's italics.

8. This proposition is examined more closely in chapter 3.

9. This notion is borrowed from a seminar with this title conducted for the Graduate Faculty of the New School for Social Research by John Caputo, winter quarter, 1995.

10. The notion of phenomenological "destruction" (*Destruktion*) appears first in Martin Heidegger's, *Being and Time*, trans. John Macquarri and Edward Robinson (New York: Harper and Row, 1962), pp. 41–49, esp. 44. There it refers to the undermining of what he calls our "naive" way of seeing and thinking Being. This is done by displaying its historic origins. In other words, for Heidegger "destruction" has an explicitly philosophical goal. I have the considerably less ambitious goal of "destroying" entities such as enemies, races, homosexuality, addiction, and so forth. Occasionally, I use the more popular word "deconstruction" to stand for this practice.

11. Husserl, *Caretesian Meditations*, pp. 33–37. See also Berger and Luckmann, *The Social Construction of Reality*, pp. 21–28.

12. This interpretation of alienation (*Entfremdung*) originates with Karl Marx. See Erich Fromm, *Marx's Concept of Man* (New York: Ungar, 1961).

13. The phrase "ceaseless reality work" is from Hugh Mehan and Houston Wood, *The Reality of Ethnomethodology* (New York: John Wiley and Sons, 1977), pp. 20–23.

14. Benjamin Whorf, *Language, Thought and Reality*, ed. and intro. John Carroll (Cambridge, MA: Massachusetts Institute of Technology, 1956), pp. 148–57, 207–19.

15. Harold Garfinkel, *Studies in Ethnomethodology* (Englewood Cliffs, NJ: Prentice-Hall, 1967).

16. Husserl, *Cartesian Meditations*, pp. 19–20.

17. See Erich Goode and Nachman Ben-Yehuda, *Moral Panics: The Social Construction of Deviance* (Cambridge, MA: Blackwell, 1994).

2

THE APOCALYPSE OF MODERNITY

Every life-world is a coherency of things. Given their nature, each life-world also has an horizon of possibilities, limits on what is imaginable and realistically doable. Because "Anglo" time is experienced as a spatial continuum, for instance, historiography is conceivable. The procession of events can be given direction, purpose, meaning. It becomes possible to escape the "eternal yesterday," to fantasize about progress, agonize about the "last days."[1]

Every life-world has in addition a "center" relative to which truth claims can be assessed, actions judged, beauty ascertained. Peripheral concerns and interests are just that. They are marginalized, viewed as irrelevant to the "important" things in life, the so-called real world.

In ancient times, world centers were represented vividly and geographically. The classic example, of course, is Babylonia's world *omphalos* or navel (the tower of Babel). This was a mud brick ziggurat linking heaven and earth and atop which the New Year's festival was conducted each spring, involving the death and resurrection of the god-king. Facsimiles of this architecture have been uncovered in Tenochtitlán, Mexico, and in the Forbidden City, heart of the Flowery States of the classic Chinese world.

THE MODERN WORLD

The modern world has its own geographic center, indeed a series of contending centers: Paris, Berlin, London, and today New York—these following a train of military victories and commercial preeminences. However, the primordial Center and unchanging measure of modernity relative to which all else is marginal is Man(kind) Itself: Its interests, Its outlook. Our's, in other words, is an *anthro*centric era. This chapter argues that the human center of modernity has destabilized and collapsed. Its fragmentation has opened space for a new revelation. I call both the fracture and what shows itself in it the Apocalypse of Modernity.

Later, I present a more thorough archaeology of modernity. Here, it is enough to date its birth to around AD 1500, and to acknowledge its paternity as having been multiple—Francis Bacon, Martin Luther, Rene Descartes, John Calvin, and Thomas Hobbes being numbered among its fathers. Each in his own way encouraged God's retreat from everyday affairs. Ironically, this was not done with the expressed purpose of denigrating the godhead, but to enliven Christian faith.

The case of Luther is typical. Besides secularizing the notion of the vocational life by elevating medicine, law, teaching, and business to statuses equal in honor to the clergy, Luther insisted on separating the affairs of the State from those of the Church. The Church, he claimed, should concern itself exclusively with matters of the spirit, the State alone with power. In divesting the Church of political responsibilities, Luther inadvertently freed the State of moral fetters in the pursuit of its own interests. It is no coincidence that following the dissemination of his writings, history's first scientifically equipped armies appeared in Lutheran Sweden, and then in the Protestant Netherlands.[2]

Bacon, Calvin, and Hobbes had comparable impacts: Bacon repudiated divine revelation as a reliable means for validating truth claims, insisting instead on direct observation; Calvin rid Christianity of practices that distracted believers from focusing solely on the Lord. Now, not only was Luther's State disenchanted but the Church was too; Hobbes completed the task of demystification by showing how governments arise from contracts entered into by men of reason to protect their own interests, not from divine appointment.

In short, God began His ineluctable "disappearance" from European affairs sometime after AD 1500, finally "dying" altogether four centuries later, his obituary being announced by Friedrich Nietzsche.[3] In God's place, Mankind arose to fill the void. Man Itself became the Center of modernity.

Historically, there have been two anthrocentrisms: that of the Left, so to say, which posits the Proletariat as humanity's true source and purpose; and that of the Right, which insists that the Volk, the Nation, or the tribe is that against which all things must be judged. As compelling (and deadly) as each of these have been, both pale in importance to conviction in the centrality of individual Selfhood. In the modern era God has been superseded not by Class or by Race (at least not for long), but by the rational, willful, self-interested Ego. It is the imperiling of *this* center that has occasioned the Apocalypse of Modernity.

THE APOCALYPSE OF MODERNITY

Around AD 1800, localized debates between free-thinking male English gentlemen (the Founding Fathers) and their French Enlightenment counterparts produced what today are celebrated, respectively, as the American Creed and the Declaration of the Rights of Man. Both announced as "self-evidently true" that insofar as they are human then each individual has claim to life, liberty, and happiness.

Slavery and imperialism posed a dilemma to these thinkers.[4] If, on the one hand, human essence was granted to Africans, Native Americans, Hindus, Polynesians, Chinese, Arabs, and Aborigines, then there would be no moral basis for their exploitation, exclusion, or excision. If, on the other hand, life, liberty, and happiness were refused them, this would require acceptance of the idea that they are little more than beasts.[5]

The consequences of the second of the dilemma's two horns are amply documented in libraries of infamy throughout Euro-America. They are summarized in a phrase still heard in extremist enclaves today: "Not everything that walks on two legs is human."

Instead, they are 'coons, rats, dogs, or worse, "mud people": denizens of darkness, frequenters of garbage heaps, dregs, excrement, to be dealt with accordingly.

Only that which is *essentially* human warrants individual rights, so the argument went. However, humanity is incumbent upon the display of reason. According to Rene Descartes, it is to think— *cogito: sum*; but the outward sign of reasoning is the capacity to read and write. To the Founding Fathers and Enlightenment philosophers, the Center of modernity is pictured as a literate two-legged animal in pursuit of its own interests. As for illiterate hominids, they are relegated in maps of early modern geographers to *terra incognita*, the earth's unexplored periphery. They are *Homo monstrosus*. Some, it is alleged, "eat their enemies, some burn them, and some mutilate them; . . . in one country the child kills his parent . . . and in another the parent eats his child."[6]

The denial of humanity to non-Europeans, however, was just one response to contact with human variety. The second, and as it turns out inestimably more important historically, has been "liberalism," the presumption that non-Europeans are themselves human. They are not simply objects of nature to be overcome, used, then discarded. They are thinking, knowing selves in their own right, hence worthy of freedom.

The possibility of humanity was granted first to those non-Europeans inhabiting the remnants of civilizations as majestic as anything in Europe, with their own monuments, cities, temples, and artworks. These in turn rested on literatures of law and saga, historical anecdote, poetry and myth: India's *dharmashastras* and Mahabharata, China's *Spring and Autumn Annals* and its commentaries and glosses, the Aztecan *Florentine Codex*.

Confrontation with civilized non-Europeans constituted an intellectual challenge of massive proportions to Westerners. How could peoples so different from ourselves (i.e., from Europeans) in language, confession, folkways, and above all in appearance be so "human"? The most attractive answer initially was simply to deny the actuality of their difference by insisting that beneath the variety of alien tastes, mores, and skin colors resides "essential man," man-as-knower (Descartes's *cogito*).[7] Regarding the Hindus, Pakastanis, Afghans, and Persians, for example, an elaborate saga was concocted demonstrating that (along with the Nordic, Germanic,

Celtic, and Greco-Roman peoples) they all derive from the same, racially superior, Indo-Aryan stock.[8] In the case of the Aztec, Mayan, and Peruvian peoples, chroniclers argued that they are descendants of the legendary Lost Tribes of Israel. Thus their civilizations are merely bizarre offshoots from European tradition.[9]

Needless to say, this way of handling human variety was considerably less satisfying when applied to the preliterate folk of Africa, Australia, and America, or most pointedly, to females. Having once admitted *these* others into the realm of humanity, the liberal was compelled to entertain the possibility that being human might mean infinitely more than Descartes's *cogito*. This is the moment when modernity's Center began to crumble.

Henry Louis Gates, Jr., tells the story this way.[10] It is late in the eighteenth-century; an 18-year-old black slave woman named Phyllis Wheatly reads from a sheaf of her own poems to a gathering of skeptical Boston elders. While the shocking event goes virtually unreported at the time, it shatters the almost universally held presumption that aboriginal folk are incapable of reason.

Wheatly, of course, is freed from her bonds. Hearing of this, other voices earlier condemned to silence now find their way to print, at first slowly and then with the gathering momentum of a tidal wave: that of the male slave, that of the Indian, the African, and the Arab. "The recording of an authentic black [Indian, African, or Arab] voice," says Gates, was "the millennial instrument of transformation through which the . . . slave [became] the ex-slave, brute animal [became] the human animal."

Now something entirely unforeseen came into being: as once stilled voices came to be published, "essential Man," modernity's rational ego, begins rupturing into a plurality of parochial "men," each with his own style of mindedness and body life: African man, Islamic man, Native American man, and so forth.[11] Today, this planetary-wide insurgency is called "identity politics." With the advent of identity politics, the centrality of Euro-American male perception, reasoning, and emotional sensibility is displaced and relativized. Descartes's *cogito* comes to be seen as merely one more situated identity, as biased and partial as the rest.

In the 1950s, simultaneously as Man disperses into "men," there appears Woman with *her* own "her-story," *her* own presumably nonmasculine way of being-in-the-world.[12] Then, within two decades Woman (meaning college-educated, middle-class, Caucasian, Euro-American female experience generalized to all females) explodes into a profusion of lower-case "women" of different races, classes, and tribal allegiances, each with *their* unique differences, each demanding recognition.[13]

As the twentieth century draws to a close, homosexuals rail against "compulsory heterosexuality," insisting that human sexual difference not be encompassed in two clumsy categories, male and female. There exist instead three, maybe more, sexualities, each of which discloses truths about human existence.[14]

In sum, as modernity's imperial destiny unfolded, it was "decentered by difference," to paraphrase Jacques Derrida. Its Center, the rational, calculating ego, lost plausibility. At that moment "linguistics invade[d] the universal problematic."[15]

Crises (from the Greek *krinein* [to split]) shatter what is taken for granted as natural, inevitable, and right. In doing so, they provide an opportunity for new insights. When posed in prophetic words, these "in-flashings," as Martin Heidegger calls them, give rise to new worlds. This paradoxical "birthing-at-the-moment-of-death" is encompassed in the Greek term "apocalypse" (*apo* = reversal + *kalyptein* = to cover). An apocalypse is not simply an ending. It is also and more importantly a beginning, an uncovering, an illumination unveiled precisely at the very moment of greatest darkness and danger. To quote Heidegger's favorite poet Hölderlin, the fracturing of the old world *is* the saving power "inasmuch as it brings the saving power out of its . . . concealed essence."[16]

In the vacuum left after God's erasure in the nineteenth century, prophets announced the Age of Man. In our era, Man Itself has come to an end.[17] In the emptiness occasioned by Man's disappearance, a new revelation shows itself. Call it the Linguistic Turn.[18]

THE LINGUISTIC TURN

With the repetition of situated, equally parochial identities—Afrocentric, homocentric, Islamic, femicentric, and so on—the suspicion has spread among reflective persons that the search for a single foundation, an eternal and universal Center, may be ultimately futile. Perhaps all that really exists is "the repetition itself," to quote Derrida again: talk, discourse, language games, words. This is what Derrida means by his rather awkward assertion that at the end of the twentieth century, linguistics has "invaded" the universal problematic. Language studies and ethnography, conversational analysis, symbolic interactionism, and semiotics have become the intellectual common denominators of our age.

Prior to this the world was seen and thought to be a coherency of things experienced alike by all sane persons. Today, it presents itself to consciousness as a "world*view*," a *life*-world, which is to say, as a language game.

Reality, once believed to have an ontology, a being, independent of its knowers, has evolved into a *linguistic construct*. It is now written as *lived*-reality, less what words describe than what words "accomplish."

Temporality, a fundamental dimension of reality, heretofore thought to be a given in the nature of things-themselves, is now understood as a *notion*, a localized theory. There is "Anglo" linear time, a parchment progressively unraveling. There is Hopi time, the same thing returning again and again.

While race is still widely thought to be a biological fact, to those influenced by Derrida's "repetition," it is written as a "*trope* of the world," a quaint (if dangerous) figure of speech, perhaps invented by Portuguese explorers—in any case, a form of talk, a conversation piece.

Our very own flesh, our sexual appetites, and our preferences, earlier believed given irrevocably in DNA, are now seen as social constructs, products of discourse. There is only the *lived*-body with its *lived*-pains and -desires.

In place of Man's being, in other words, little remains but "*concepts* of man," metaphors and anecdotes, some demeaning and others honorific: the Marxist concept of man (*homo laborans*), man as playful animal (*homo ludens*), man as creature (i.e., as product of a Creator), man as cyborg, and so forth. Indeed, our very core, which Freud named the Id, the It, which for him was a cesspool of lubricous sexuality and destructiveness has dissolved into words. To his latest translator, the Id is but "dream *language*," with a structure analogous to puns and double-entendres.

In sum, in our era "all that is solid [has] melt[ed] into the air."[19] Everything that before had provided a ground on which to stand, a foundation, has been "destructured" into linguistic conventions. The space occasioned by the decentering of modernity beckons us to yield to the void. Instead of forcing things into prefit boxes, we are asked to "let beings be," "to give them ear," to let them reveal themselves to us. This is the revelation showing itself at the "moment of greatest danger" today—one this book seeks to recount.

NOTES

1. Eric Voegelin, *Israel and Revelation* (Baton Rouge: Louisiana State University Press, 1956), pp. 21–33, 111–33.

2. James Aho, *Religious Mythology and the Art of War* (Westport, CT: Greenwood Press, 1981), pp. 194–217.

3. Friedrich Nietzsche, "The Gay Science," in *The Portable Nietzsche*, trans. and ed. Walter Kaufmann (New York: Vintage Books, 1954), sec. 123.

4. Gunnar Myrdal, *The American Dilemma* (New York: Harper and Brothers, 1944).

5. Charles Lemert, "Dark Thoughts about the Self," in *Social Theory and the Politics of Identity*, ed. Craig Calhoun (Cambridge, MA: Blackwell, 1994), p. 107.

6. Georges Louis Leclerc Buffon, *A Natural History of the Globe, of Man*, . . . (New York: Leavitt & Allen, 1857 [1749]), p. 132.

7. Until the early 1960s this historiographic style enjoyed widespread acceptance in Euro-American intellectual circles. For an example see William McNeill, *The Rise of the West* (Chicago: University of Chicago Press, 1963).

8. Leon Poliakov, *The Aryan Myth* (New York: Basic Books, 1971).

9. This is the basis of the Book of Mormon, one of the holy books for The Church of Jesus Christ, Latter-day Saints (Mormon).

10. Henry Louis Gates, Jr., "Race as the Trope of the World," in *Race, Writing and Difference*, ed. Henry Louis Gates, Jr. (Chicago: University of Chicago Press, 1986), pp. 4–13.

11. Molefi Asante, *The Afrocentric Idea* (Philadelphia: Temple University Press, 1987). Each of these lesser beings has themselves splintered into smaller units. For example, see Edward Said's critique of Oriental essence in *Orientalism* (New York: Vintage Books, 1978).

12. The classic statement is Simone de Beauvoir, *The Second Sex*, trans. H. M. Parshley (New York: Vintage Books, 1949).

13. Elisabeth Spelman, *Inessential Woman* (Boston: Beacon Press, 1989).

14. Adrienne Rich, "Compulsory Heterosexuality and Lesbian Existence," in *Powers of Desire*, ed. A. Sitnow, C. Stanwell, and S. Thompson (New York: Monthly Review Press, 1983).

15. Jacques Derrida, *Writing and Difference*, trans. and intro. Alan Bass (Chicago: University of Chicago Press, 1978), pp. 278–82.

16. Martin Heidegger, "The Turning," in *The Question of Technology and Other Essays*, trans. and intro. William Lovitt (New York: Harper and Row, 1977), p. 42.

17. Michael Clifford, "Postmodern Thought and the End of Man," in *The Question of the Other*, ed. Arleen Dallery and Charles Scott (Albany: State University of New York Press, 1989), pp. 213–21.

18. "The Linguistic Turn" is borrowed from Charles Lemert. It is not the only revelation making its appearance on the heels of Man's decentering. Perhaps even more important is the planetwide resurgence of fundamentalisms. The planned six-volume Fundamentalism Project out of the University of Chicago acknowledges the significance of such movements in our era. The first volume was published in 1991 by the University of Chicago Press.

19. Marshall Berman, *All That Is Solid Melts into the Air* (New York: Simon and Schuster, 1982). The title for this book is taken from Karl Marx and Friedrich Engels, *The Manifesto of the Communist Party* (New York: International Publishers, 1930 [1848]). The rest of the sentence reads: "all that is holy is profaned, and man is at last compelled to face with sober sense, his real conditions of life, and his relations with his kind."

3

WORDS AND WORLDS

WORDS

Bees "dance." They whirl first clockwise then counterclockwise, occasionally accompanied by an antennae-connected train of fellow foragers.[1] Depending on the speed of the rounds, and the direction faced by the lead dancer at the outset of her performance, other workers in the hive can locate hidden pollen sources up to three miles away. The various whirlings and abdomen waggings mean the same things to all the bees. Hence, each is able to align her own minuscule efforts at gathering food with others for the benefit of all.

Human beings talk. Their conversations vocalize private experiences, crystallizing them in publicly accessible form. You hear me and so become aware of what is "on my mind." I *also* hear myself and my thoughts and feelings become clearer to *me* as well—but never entirely. "The spoken word is pregnant with meaning," yet it never quite contains the inner thought. Every attempt to verbally "close our hand on the thought . . . [leaves] only a bit of verbal material in our fingers."[2] As a result I may not always know more than you about what I am thinking and feeling. Nevertheless, to the extent you and I do understand each other's words, we can work, pray, and play together. Not that we communicate *just* by words. There are also the *ways* we talk: our tone of voice, the rapidity of our expressions, our loudness, and our inflection. More importantly, we do not just converse verbally. We also "talk" with our silences, with our interruptions, our physiognomies and postures, with our hands and faces, with our costumery, and the props we position around ourselves. Included among these are the kinds of people we are seen with, our room furnishings, the foods we consume, and our musical tastes. Even the distances we keep from others and the ways we move through space—whether by foot or by vehicle, whether by private or public conveyance, whether by Chevrolet or BMW—tell others things about us. "The fact is that culture itself is a tissue of codes, a complex system of signs whose meanings may not always lie right on the surface."[3] In other words, the entirety of culture can be "read" as one would any "text": theme parks like Disneyland and Sea World, "Wheel of Fortune," "Nightline," Gucci shoes, Cabbage Patch dolls, sushi, and Sid Vicious.[4]

Speaking is conventional. To be understood it must proceed according to linguistic rules. Competent speakers need not be conscious of these rules, any more than they must be aware of the normative basis of their own dress preferences or culinary tastes. Whether speakers are conscious of them or not, linguistic rules force their thought patterns, feelings, and perceptions into preset grooves. Like all artifacts, in other words, languages boomerang back to "re-create" their creators. We use languages and they in turn "use" us. This is not to say that languages (or cultures in general) mechanically reproduce people, imprinting their formal structures onto plastic material, a view promulgated in vulgar sociology. Rather, words and grammars are actively "appropriated." As they are used to articulate human needs and desires or to facilitate human interests, their meanings and requirements are challenged, debated, clarified, and modified.

Take the racial signifier "white." Originally, it had a scope of extension limited to Anglo-Saxons. Today, the term encompasses Scandinavians, Celts, and Germans—who Benjamin Franklin once claimed were no more able to adopt British customs "than they can acquire our Complexion"—as well as Finns, Russians, Italians, Spaniards, Portuguese, and Greeks.[5] As recently as 1920, the latter were widely considered "colored" folk and as having "physiog-

nom[ies] . . . [that] unmistakably proclaim inferiority of type."
"That they are morally below the races of northern Europe," says
period sociologist Edward Ross, "is as certain as any social fact."[6]
Because it confers obvious privileges, however, various American
minorities have insisted on appropriating "white" to themselves.
In response, nativist groups like the Know-Nothing party, the
American Protection Association, and the Ku Klux Klan have
fought to keep the "true" meaning of the term from being "di-
luted." More than once their counterarguments have been posed
in the language of guns, torches, and nooses. It is a comment on
the persuasiveness of minority orators that contemporary "white"
racialist groups now admit to their membership rolls people with
Irish, German, Spanish, Italian, Albanian, Polish, and Finnish sur-
names: all working together to defend "white America" against
"invading hordes of alien mongrels." It is not inconceivable, given
the prestige-value of the term, that through a process of claims
making and concession eventually *all* Americans may one day be
understood to be essentially "white."

Similar examples could be cited concerning the meanings of "real
man," "Christian," "hero," and "death." Indeed, there is no end
of examples. As Brian Fay recently said, language is more accurately pictured as a never-ending process than as a concrete structure of rules.[7] However this may be, such structures must always
remain to some extent privileged phenomenologically. For it is
these that make the contested appropriations just mentioned possible in the first place. The most vicious denunciations and scandalous pronouncements, the most subversive musics (e.g., rap and
rock), and the vilest pornographies are understood only against the
backdrop of a preexisting linguistic (or cultural) order. This being
so, a few comments on this order are fitting.

Semantics

Semantics is that aspect of a language concerned with meanings.
Technically, every sign has both a *de*notative and a much more
important *con*notative meaning. The first is the thing or idea to
which the word-sound points: for example, "boy" to a male child.
The second refers to the broader meaning-resonance of the term,
or to what Ferdinand de Saussure, considered to be the founder of

modern semantics, calls its "value": the images, feelings, judgments, and so forth conjured by the word. Among other notions, for example, "boyhood" suggests immaturity, diminutiveness, and (according to Roget's *Thesaurus*) puppyness. Thus, it implies something cute, cuddly, and playful, but prone to trouble.

Saussure claims that meaning-values always emerge from the "play of differences" within a language.[8] Only by understanding the oppositions and equivalences between all the words of a language can the complete significance of any one be fully grasped. Comprehension of "puppy," for example, presupposes familiarity with "dog," but also with "cat," "wolf," "house trained," "spayed," "nice," "dirty," "fur," and "wild." The meanings of each of these in turn rest on their connections to others, and so on without end.

As just pointed out, meanings are rarely invariant over time. Semanticists speak of symbols "competing" with each other for territory, "encroaching" on each other's space, and occasionally "eliminating" their competition. Dwight Bolinger writes of how the Middle Dutch *steken*, from which we get the word "stick" (to pierce or cause to adhere), "invaded" and eventually "colonized" itself in several languages.[9] First, the French borrowed it, turning the verb *steken* into the noun *etiquet*. This was then "imported" into English as "ticket," that which is tacked to a surface. In the hands of the Spanish, *etiquet* became *etiqueta*, the rules of conduct posted (tacked to the wall) at court functions, the "ticket" or the correct thing to do. Finally, the French took up the Spanish variation, rendering *etiqueta* as *etiquette* (the rules of courtly propriety), a term absorbed into English.

The semantic reach of words can become so extensive that by taking time to understand them the depths of entire life-worlds can be comprehended. Take the Spanish verb *chingar*.[10] The Mexican poet and historian Octavio Paz tells us that *chingar* comes from *chingaste*, which is equivalent to the English "sediment" or "residue." *Chingaste* is a corruption of the Aztecan *xinachtle* (garden seed) or *xinaxli* (fermented cactus juice). This explains the term's associations in Mexico with alcohol, a product of fermentation (*chinguere*); in Peru, Ecuador, and Chile with "tavern" (*chingana*); and in Spain with "drunkeness" (*chingar*).

Paz goes on to say that sediments or dregs are "leftovers" and are typically experienced as worthless. Hence, *chingar* also points to a sense failure. For example, *chinga* are things that do not work right; *chingarse*, disappointments or people who disappoint. In Argentina *la vestido chingado* is a torn dress.

That which is devalued in one sense may also be devalued in another. Hence, *chingar* also implies moral negativity. To be less than worthy is to be bad; and to be bad is to be guilty. It is to deserve scorn, ridicule, mockery, molestation. This is the reasoning behind the colloquial phrase "to *chingar*" someone. It is to prod them, goad them, incite them, frustrate them to the point of rage. One whose responses can be controlled by another in this way is less than completely human, less than a man. In effect such a person is misery itself, dust, emptiness, of no account. In sum, *chingar* is a "magical word," says Paz, a term the subtle ambivalence of which provides the basis of "poetry within reach of everyone" in the Hispanic world. It is the symbolic master key that unlocks the secret solitude and sullenness of the Mexican soul.

Like any life-world, that of the prototypical Mexican contains many divisions, one of the most basic being that between *chingada* and *chingones*. *Chingadas* are the victims of *chingar*, the goading mentioned above. They are passive, defenseless, open, weak. They are "women of both sexes," the "bitten" and humiliated, those whose private spaces, lives, and bodies are penetrated. To use the familiar English expression, *chingadas* are those who are "screwed." Above their prostrated form strut *chingones*, real men.

Like beasts who stalk their prey at night, *chingones* "bite." They sting and gash. They not only inflict physical pain; they also demean and humiliate their victims. They are active, inscrutable, cruel, unfeeling. The *chingone* plots (*chingaquedito*); he defies (*chingadera*); he breaks (*chingo*) others by committing *chingaderas* on them. He is the *macho* man, the big power man (*gran chingone*).

Business magnates, Don Juans, politicians, generals, and large landowners are *gran chingones*. They attract the attention of females and sycophants (*lambiscones* = lickers). In contrast, to be known as *chingada* is to be degraded in the vilest way. It is to be known as *nada*, nothing, dirt, the lees that remain after tea, garbage: something to be discarded. (The reader will want to keep this in mind when discussion turns to the attributes of enemies in a later chapter.)

What, then, is to be made of this collective hurrah, heard on the 15th of September, Mexican independence day? *"Viva Mexico. Hijos* [sons] *de la Chingada!"* Paz says that this exhortation expresses the core of the Mexican collective unconscious. It condemns the Spanish conquest of Mexico, an event symbolized in popular legend by Hernando Cortez's rape of the Aztecan princess Dona Marina. She is *la Chingada*, the archetypal violated Mother. The Mexican people are nationally unified by virtue of their descent from the penultimate Victim of Spanish colonial rule. There is more to it than this. Insofar as *chingada* is abject negativity, then the shout also affirms that the Mexican people have arisen from nothingness. They are a self-generated folk who, although connected with the past, have no debt to it. They are their own creation, responsible solely to themselves. Neither exclusively Spanish nor Indian, "his [the Mexican's] beginnings are in his own self," says Paz. Mexico conceives itself as a negation of its negative roots, an affirmation of itself.

Syntax

Effective conversation not only presupposes a grasp of individual meanings, but also an ability to combine words into sensible communications. "Tall dark men fight ferociously" makes sense to speakers of English. The same words, with the same references, but positioned in reverse order produce gibberish: "Ferociously fight men dark tall."

One grammatical rule in English is that meaningful sentences must contain both a subject and a predicate, a substantive for every verb. "Rains," for example, by itself is an incomplete sentence. Speakers wishing to make themselves clear must therefore add (and sometimes invent entirely fictitious) subject terms in order to play the language game: "cloud," or more revealingly, "it," as in "It rains." According to Benjamin Whorf, the Hopi do not have this convention. Where Anglos are required to combine noun and verb into the sentence "Light flashes" to be understood, the Hopi are only made to utter the verb "flashes" (*rephi*).[11] The Hopi would insist that to talk otherwise is to be redundant, says Whorf. After all, the light and the flash are identical.

Whorf goes on to argue that what is at stake here is far more than a matter of linguistic efficiency. The very assumptions of Western metaphysics, he claims, which until recently were held to be universal and eternal, are in effect generalizations from the requirement that every predicate have a subject, every verb a noun. That is, because speakers of Western languages (including English, French, German, and Russian) are grammatically admonished to find nouns for their verbs, says Whorf, they are tricked into imagining that reality itself is comprised of static things and active processes. Thus, where there is blowing (a verb) there also must be wind (a noun), where there is falling (a process) there also must be rain (a thing), where there is passing there also must be time. Predictably, every Western metaphysician from Plato to Kant has insisted that reality is divisible into two basic elements: matter and motion, space and time, form and content, and so forth. This is so even though, as the Hopi might say, there can be no wind without blowing (or vice versa), no rain without (it) falling, no time without the passing of events, or to express it technically, no matter without motion.

By not having to identify a noun for every verb in composing their sentences, Whorf claims that the Hopi people come closer to experiencing the "flowing face of nature in its motion, . . . and changing form." Hopi metaphysics, that is to say, is presumably closer to actuality than our own metaphysics. The reader should bear in mind that apart from telling the reader how nature "actually" is, Whorf, like many anthropologists, may have romanticized his subjects.

LANGUAGE AND MIND

Two attributes of mindedness are thinking and seeing, or as they are called technically, conceiving and perceiving. Both, if not entirely determined by language, as is sometimes supposed, at least depend a great deal on language. Thus, infants and aphasiacs, both of whom are incapable of speech, necessarily have diminished mental capacities.[12] To the degree that peoples' languages differ, so do the contents of their minds differ, and hence the assertion that the mind is a "social construct."[13]

At any moment we are inundated with sensations: radio static, hall voices, machine hums, footsteps, the aromas of ozone, perfume, and wet dog hair, tire squeals and horn honks, sirens, the sticky feeling of fingers on keyboards, overly constricting trousers, dull aches, and visual sensations: trees outside the window, dust on the sill, shades askew, open file cabinet drawers, mud on the floor, and papers and books strewn about. Typically, however, we move into this profusion of sensation in what Norman Denzin and others call the "categorical attitude."[14] We begin ordering it with the aid of linguistic categories. What before was confused, which is to say, "fused together," is broken down, regrouped, "nominized." Some of the sensations are gathered together while being separated from the rest.

"Conceiving" comes from the Latin (*con* = together + *capere* = to take or seize). To conceive is to arrest, to "apprehend" the motility of sensation, to group it, and to judge its significance. This is reflected colloquially in phrases like, "Can you 'grasp' what I'm getting at?" "Can you 'get a handle' on it?" "Yes, I 'get' it; it is 'comprehendible.' " That which is "caught" is the sensation; what "grasps" it is the word. The same can be said for *per*ceiving. Seeing is not merely sensations impinging on the retina of the eyeball, anymore than hearing is the response of membranes and cartilage to sound waves. Both seeing and hearing, in addition, regiment nerve impulses. Both give meaning to sensation by categorizing it. The categories themselves are the components of language, its verbs and nouns. To be without language is to be truly sightless and deaf.

In English there exists the generic category "camel." In Arabic, while there is no single term equivalent to camel, there are six thousand words for different kinds of camels, distinguished by function, breed, presumed nobility of lineage, sex, age, state of pregnancy, and so on. The complexity of the camel realm bespeaks the pivotal importance they occupy in bedouin economics.[15] What English-speakers ordinarily take to be a single animal is in bedouin thinking a cacophony of finely graded differences.

Again, while modern zoology recognizes ten major animal divisions, the Dalabon, an aboriginal folk residing in northern Australia, have only three. There are *djen* (fish), *ma:n* (insects, snakes, birds, dogs, and small marsupials), and *guin* (large marsupials).[16] Zoology groups animals on the basis of their structural and physiological likenesses. Dalabon taxonomy distinguishes between food sources, and between these in terms of location, ease of entrapment, snare types, danger, and so forth. Thus, while to the zoologist insects, snakes, birds, and dogs are radically different, to the Dalabon they are essentially alike.

This is not to suggest that Anglo-Americans are unable to tell the difference between one camel and another, or that the Dalabon could not, if asked, segregate dogs from insects and birds. This would be as absurd as claiming, as one critic recently did in jest, that people without a word for orgasm can not have one. This having been said, however, it is true that the task of discriminating between camels is less efficient linguistically for English-speakers than it is for bedouins, requiring elaborate combinations of modifiers. It takes less energy to recall a single Arabic sound-word than it does the phrase "double-humped, female camel, descended from such and such oasis herd, of seven years, ready to give birth."[17]

Lived-Time

There is time-itself, the sensation of one thing following another. Then there is *lived*-time, how this procession is thought and seen. Lived-time is partly a linguistic artifact.

English has three verbal tenses: past, representing "once but no more"; present, "now"; and future, "yet to be": "He ran." "He runs." "He will run." In this grammar, time is experienced as a thing with spatial extension, or to use the image introduced earlier, as a scroll or tape measure steadily unwinding. As a spatial phenomenon, time is thus thought capable of being partitioned into units of equal length—days, seconds, years—by which specific events can be located.

Lived-time for the Hopi is different; this is reflected in their grammar.[18] First, Hopi has no tenses in the strict sense, only what Benjamin Whorf calls "tensors," verb suffixes, and just two of these. Tensors, he says, allow hearers to distinguish the type of information required to validate a speaker's assertion. They do not serve to place events on a time-scroll.

Take the Hopi equivalent for "run," *wari*. *Wari* is equivalent to the sentence "He ran." It also stands for "He runs." *Wari* has the same verb tensor in both cases because both are reports capable of being validated by observation. Past and present are not conceivable to the Hopi people in the same way they are to us, as entirely separate dimensions.

As for assertions implying expectancy, the closest concept in Hopi grammar to the English future tense requires the addition of the suffix *-ni*; "He will run," for example, is rendered as *wari-ni*. Again, the reason for the different verb ending is not that "yet to be's" reside in a separate temporal dimension, but that confirmation of expectancies requires different information than claims about past and present.

The upshot of this, according to Whorf, is that Hopi time is not something moving from the past, through the present, into the future. Indeed, time is not a noun at all, a word to which material metaphors can be affixed. Rather, it is an adverb, a verb ending, signifying the "getting later" of an event. To say it in reverse, time is the manifesting of acts, some further along in process than others.

Whorf insists that enframing time as a verb instead of as a noun is ontologically "truer" to time-itself. There is no need to go that far here. I do not want to be misunderstood as claiming that the Hopi are incapable of discriminating between events that in English are known as occurring in the present and the past, or that they cannot count the passage of days as speakers of English do. Hopi is a Uto-Aztecan language. Among other things, the Aztecs were renowned for their detailed calendar. The most that can be granted Whorf is that linguistically some operations concerning time may have to be done "less efficiently" in Hopi than in English, requiring the use of novel word combinations. By the same token, while it may take the skill of a minor poet to enframe time in English as action "ceaselessly unfolding," that is, as an adverb instead of a noun, it can be done. Language may help structure our experience of the world, but it does not entirely determine it.

LANGUAGE AND REALITY

If the mind's functions are assembled at least partly by words, and if what we see, hear, think, and recall is reality-for-us, lived-reality, then the implication is obvious: the practical everyday world is partly a linguistic accomplishment. There are three different senses in which this is true. Failure to distinguish between them has been a source of perennial confusion in popular sociology.

First, it is by means of words that sensations are brought to our attention as identifiable things such as squirrels, earthquakes, or rain. Having once been identified we can collaborate effectively toward them. In this way shared language is essential to the existence of an orderly, predictable life-world. Nevertheless, it is a serious mistake to say that words actually create the ontologies, the very beings, of squirrels, earthquakes, and rain. These, obviously, are "already there," independent of human consciousness, awaiting names to disclose them. "Symbols do not create cats and dogs and evening stars," says John Searle. *"They create only the possibility of referring to cats, dogs, and evening stars in a publicly accessible way."*[19]

When Copernicus formally announced that the earth was a "planet" instead of an unmoved cosmic "center," this did not result in heavenly bodies suddenly changing their courses after 1543. Likewise, the internal dynamics of substances remained what they always had been even after Lavoisier saw "oxygen" where before Priestly had seen only "dephlogistinated air." Words do not make the physicalilty of things. However, they do disclose (some of) their qualities (while simultaneously veiling others), and in so doing open horizons of possibility in dealing with them. After Copernicus's and Lavoisier's discoveries, the instruments used by astronomers and chemists were re-engineered. This made it possible to visualize and think things differently, to calculate new equations, to make new predictions, and to confront new puzzles—in short, the ways in which the world was "lived," how it was experienced, altered. Phenomenologically, after Copernicus and Lavoisier, astronomers and chemists began working in new worlds.[20]

There is a second way in which words accomplish worlds. Due to their semantic complexity, most words can be used figuratively, not just to disclose (aspects of) what is already there ontologically, but also to add "something more" to their being. Take the depiction of the woman next door as a "kitten" (or as a "vixen," or as a "dog," or as having a "heavenly body"). Seen this way, words most definitely *can* "create" cats and dogs and evening stars. This is not just inconsequential word-play. For again, how a thing is inscribed "poetically" bears directly on how it is experienced, and thus what it is for all intents and purposes phenomenologically. This is a second way in which words accomplish the world.

Finally, words do not just disclose what is already there. They do not merely hyperbolize it. Words can also *constitute* things-themselves out of virtually nothing. "I do," when pronounced in certain circumstances, is sufficient for a kind of reality, marriage, to come into being. The words do not describe what is already there; they make it be there in the first place. The same can be said for war and peace, guilt and innocence, graduations, laws, presidents, and citizenship: all of these are made out of what John Austin calls "performative utterances."[21]

There is little in thin, finely inscribed, dyed cloth paper by itself that dictates that it should count as money. Other things could, and have, served just as well: cowry shells, rare pebbles, cigarettes, silver coins, plastic. What turns stuff into money is formal documentation of the fact by properly designated authorities, who themselves have been "made" so by a series of pronouncements. Again, what differentiates a legal sale from theft is announcement of the fact by bills, signed credit extensions, and the exchange of currency.

During the Catholic sacrament of the mass, wine and unleavened bread are said to be "transubstantiated," that is, literally turned into the blood and body of Christ—this by the ritual utterance of certain phrases by a man "ordained" to the job. His ordination in turn is accomplished by the recitation of other words by still others similarly ordained. While the physical chemistries of the bread and wine are not altered by the words, what they are to believers *is* changed, and thus what they are as *lived*-objects.

It helps very little to dismiss actions such as these as "magic," as Max Weber, among others, does. For if the Catholic sacramentary is magical, then so are large portions of the life-world. After all, the colored paper referred to above is not changed physically by Treasury Department officials declaring it legal tender. The physiologies of the couple above are not altered when they are pronounced man and wife. As an Hindu adept might say, it is all verbal sleight of hand, *maya*, illusion. (The Sanskrit word *maya* has the same root as "magic.") At least in respect to its social and ideal objects, then, much of the life-world is a multilayered complex of assigned statuses, duties, and privileges devised from little more than words.

CONCLUSION

The most important things in the life-world, of course, are those right here, persons: you, me, and others. Like other things, persons too become manifest in the course of conversation. They emerge from a mosaic of spontaneous labelings and ritualized judgments, written and oral, conferred both verbally and bodily, issued by themselves and by others. In a sense, then, persons are so because they are "said" to be so. Let me be clear about this. Person-referential sayings not only *authorize* a certain animal (us) to claim moral responsibilities and rights; they also *reveal* us as being by nature already worthy of personhood. Words do not just "make" humanity; they reconfirm it.

NOTES

1. Karl von Frisch, *The Dancing Bees*, trans. Dora Ilse (London: Reader's Union/Methuen, 1955).
2. Maurice Merleau-Ponty, "On the Phenomenology of Language," in *Phenomenology, Language and Sociology*, ed. John O'Neill (London: Heinemann, 1974), p. 86.
3. Jack Solomon, *The Signs of Our Times* (New York: Harper and Row, 1988), p. 2.
4. See Marshall Blonsky, *On Signs* (Baltimore, MD: Johns Hopkins University Press, 1985) and Arthur A. Berger, *Signs in Contemporary Culture* (New York: Longman, 1984).
5. For an example of race whitening, see Noel Ignatiev, *How the Irish Became "White"* (New York: Routledge, 1994).
6. Edward A. Ross, *The Old World and the New* (New York: Century, 1914), pp. 286–96.

7. Brian Fay, *Contemporary Philosophy of Social Science* (Cambridge, MA: Blackwell, 1996), pp. 55–63.

8. Ferdinand de Saussure, *Course in General Semantics*, trans. Wade Baskin, ed. Charles Baly and Albert Sechehaye (New York: Harper-Collins, 1965), pp. 111–17.

9. Dwight Bolinger, *Aspects of Language* (New York: Harcourt, Brace and World, 1968), p. 108.

10. Octavio Paz, *The Labyrinth of Solitude: Life and Thought in Mexico*, trans. Lysander Kemp (New York: Grove Press, 1961), pp. 73–86.

11. Benjamin Whorf, *Language, Thought and Reality*, ed. and intro. John Carroll (Cambridge, MA: Massachusetts Institute of Technology Press, 1956), pp. 207–19. As critics of Whorf have pointed out, English also permits one-word sentences: "Scat!" "Rain." "What?" To make an otherwise good point Whorf exaggerates the grammatical differences between English and Hopi. On this, see Einar Haugen, "Linguistic Relativity: Myths and Methods," in *Language and Thought: Anthropological Issues*, ed. W. C. McCormack and S. A. Wurm (The Hague: Mouton, 1977), pp. 11–28.

12. Both "infant" and "aphasia" literally mean nonspeaking. The first is a Latin derivative, the second comes from Greek. For observations on aphasia and mindlessness, see Alfred Lindesmith, Anselm Strauss, and Norman Denzin, *Social Psychology*, 6th ed. (Englewood Cliffs, NJ: Prentice-Hall, 1988), pp. 101–6.

13. Jeff Coulter, *The Social Construction of Mind: Studies in Ethnomethodology and Linguistic Philosophy* (Totowa, NJ: Rowan and Littlefield, 1979).

14. Lindesmith, Strauss, and Denzin, *Social Psychology*, pp. 54–57.

15. Otto Klineberg, *Social Psychology*, rev. ed. (New York: Holt, Rinehart & Winston, 1954), p. 50.

16. Kenneth Maddock, *The Australian Aborigines* (Harmondsworth, UK: Penguin, 1974). For other examples, see Brent Berlin, *Ethnobiological Classification* (Princeton, NJ: Princeton University Press, 1992) and Roy Ellen and David Reason, eds., *Classifications in Their Social Context* (New York: Academic Press, 1979).

17. The technical term for this is "codability." Code words facilitate communication and enhance cooperation. This is why the more relevant a category is for a group and the more frequently it is used, the more codable (shorter) it becomes. "Television" evolves into "TV"; "emergency medical technician" into "EMT"; and "electronically transmitted facsimile" into "fax." The tendency to invent more efficient ways to communicate is a major source of in-group jargons.

18. Whorf, *Language, Thought and Reality*, pp. 156–57.

19. John Searle, *The Construction of Social Reality* (New York: Free Press, 1975), p. 75.

20. Thomas Kuhn, *The Structure of Scientific Revolutions*, 2d ed. enl. (Chicago: University of Chicago Press, 1970), p. 118. Kuhn equivocates. On this page he insists that Lavoisier works in a new world. Later, he says that "whatever he may then see, the scientist is still looking at the same world" (p. 129). Cf. p. 135.

21. John Austin, *How To Do Things with Words* (New York: Oxford University Press, 1965).

4

ME

"Me" is what you and I are conscious of myself being. "Me" is what is "in the light" about myself. It is how I am experienced; and how I am experienced is precisely what I am as a specific thing in the life-world.

This chapter has three goals. The first is to account for the emergence of "me" in the world; the second is to delineate its features. This in turn should accomplish the third goal, to destabilize the conviction that "me" is given in the nature of things-themselves.

A HISTORY OF EGO

The autonomous, sovereign, allegedly self-made me, otherwise known as ego, has appeared several times in history—to name just three: during the third Pharonic dynasty (ca. 3000 BC), in Greece between 1500 and 500 BC, and in post-Renaissance Europe (ca. AD 1300 to our era). According to Erich Neumann, two factors favoring its appearance have been men's groups separate from extended matrilineal family units and patriarchal marriage.[1] Prior to these arrangements consciousness of self was circumscribed by the mystique of blood and sexuality, and by the rhythms of plant life. Here, "me" is indistinguishable from the collective miasma, the We. The legend of the Terrible Mother who consumes her own children—*vagina dentata* (the toothed vagina)—expresses this truth. In Jewish folklore she is known as the devouring succubus, Lilith. The comparable ancient Greek figures are Lamia, the devourer, and Empusa, blood drinker.

With the rise of men's groups apart from the matriarchate, however, a new mythology showed itself. This is the heroic saga of the warrior-son (e.g., Asshur or Marduk) who slays the mother-goddess (Tiamat) along with her consort Kingu, and then fabricates the world from their body parts. Analogous tales recite Indra's destruction of the serpent Vritra and Thor's battle with the green-scaled Grendel Worm. In various ways, at least so Neumann claims, these tales all acknowledge the reality of males slashing themselves free from the nurturing-swallowing entanglements of the Great Round to experience themselves as independent, self-governing actors.

Although Neumann fails to address it, Christianity has also lent support to ego-consciousness, both through its theology of individual salvation and by its sacramental practices. In late medieval Catholicism the most important of these was the rite of penance, or as it came to be known, confession.[2]

To receive priestly absolution of their sins, penitents were required to confess each vice by genus, species, and number (including those never acted upon, but merely thought or wished). In addition they were obligated to situate each in time and place, to reveal whether it was done alone or with others, and to characterize the statuses of those others—this together with a painstaking recounting of the motives for their transgressions. To facilitate the procedure conscientious Catholics began keeping confessional ledgers, in which the moral and theological sins were written down on each folio page with the days of the week numbered across the top. From these their spiritual development could be traced, and "data" cited for the diaries and autobiographies for which this time in history is famous. Occasionally, the rules of confession drove penitents to such an exacting awareness of their internal states that they began falling prey to a nervous condition known in Canon Law as "scrupulosity," an over-exaggerated sense of personal responsibility for the events around them (from "scruple," the smallest unit of Roman measurement).[3]

Set up to humble the confessor, then, penance sometimes had

the effect of feeding his or her vanity. Nevertheless, even the most self-obsessed Catholics knew that they were lovingly embraced by a mystery infinitely greater than themselves, Mother Church. This had the effect, at least on most believers, of tempering grandiose ego pretensions. It was therefore left to secular jurisprudence to complete the project of ego enhancement.

As Emile Durkheim has shown, civil statutes that protect citizens against trespass not only legitimize individualism; but they also back up its claims with the power of the state.[4] Laws against libel and slander, together with rights of private property, and guarantees of free speech, conscience, religion, and due process, permanently hoist "me" out of the Great Chain of Being to stand on its own two feet as a self-actualizing, immeasurably precious thing. This is the milieu out of which Rene Descartes's self-certain ego would emerge, a notion later refined by Edmund Husserl into the so-called Transcendent Ego. This, recall, is the world-constituting Self, that which resides at the very center of the modern world.

To summarize, it can be said that far from being given naturally at birth, ego-consciousness is a product of specific historical circumstances—mythic fable, ritual discourse, and law. "Me" becomes the thing it is depending on the conversational context in which it appears.

CONVERSATION AND THE SELF

"Ontogeny recapitulates phylogeny": the embryology of the human fetus repeats the evolution of the species, transforming itself in the womb from protozoan into fish, from reptile into mammal, and from primate into infant. Psychological development follows a similar pattern: the emergence of ego-consciousness at a personal level recalls what has transpired historically.

Analogous to Neumann's typification of egolessness amidst the swamp of undifferentiated sensuality, at birth the infant is conscious, but not of itself. It is con-fused with its surroundings. It is subject to sensations, but unaware of their various causes. Only after acquiring a language can the child parcel out the sensations, identifying them as separate things.[5] Words are the tools with which the world is carved.

Semantics and Self

Many linguists believe that the first word-sound universally uttered is that formed most easily by the infant's mouth, "ma-ma." Supposedly, this is followed by the harder sound "ba-ba." Whatever the case, as John Hewitt observes, the infant's announcement of these words is a "momentous event."[6] For with it not only does the child begin appropriating the world, *the world begins appropriating the child.*

At this stage, we might say, the infant's life-world consists of only one or two things, ma-ma and ba-ba, plus background noise. Furthermore, the range of application of "ma-ma" may not correspond exactly to adult usage. However, through the tactical deployment of coos and hugs, errors are soon corrected. Meanwhile, the infant learns to associate other sensations with additional terms. Among these is its own name. Again, while the name may be pronounced and applied incorrectly at first, the child soon learns to limit its extension to sensations issuing from the surface of its body-sack inward.

Personal names point to particular entities; but they also come freighted with semantic baggage the child may be required to carry: the memory of a beloved aunt or grandmother, an event or virtue (Running Deer, Harmony, Happy), a Christian saint, or an Old Testament character. As the child takes on the name, the associated baggage is hoisted to its shoulders as well. To repeat the paradox: as the child possesses the world, the world possesses the child.

In no predictable sequence other words follow, and with them more entities appear. Not only does the infant's world grow in size, but also in complexity; simultaneously, its sense of self grows firmer. There are relationship words, for example, the most important being possessive pronouns like "my" and "mine." The child's experimental, occasionally tearfully mistaken, use of these—in fights with other children over toys, or after spankings by mother for getting into "her" things—enables the child to begin demarcating arenas over which it has control. In addition to this, they enable the child to distinguish between that most truly its own and that which it can merely dispose of as it sees fit. Private spheres of power are crucial to modern ego-sense; such arenas are sculpted from sensation by means of possessive pronouns.

The child learns that there are subtle differences in degree of mine-ness. "My toys" can and should be shared with "friends"; some of "my things" are "no-nos." Only the child itself can touch them, and then only in specific ways at particular times. At least in middle-class America, these include the child's genitals. The reader hardly needs to be reminded of how fragile knowledge of physical inviolability is. We are not born with the concept of "abuse," that our bodies can somehow be illegitimately invaded. Practices inflicted on children that today would risk a jail sentence—penial subincision, labial extirpation, elongation of the clitoris, the daubing of girls' genitals with honey—have been honored at other times and places.[7]

Suzanne Bunkers writes of a little girl, Emily, who offers to tell her mother about a "game" she and Eric play, but only if the mother "promises not to tell Daddy." He will ground them if he finds out, Emily warns. Eric, she says, takes off his clothes, then her's. He fondles and kisses her genitals and she does the same with his. The horrified mother reminds Emily of how her "private parts" are "yours alone and nobody has the right to touch them except you." Emily, exasperated, retorts, "But Mommy, he's my *brother*."[8] The point is that having "privates" that are off-limits even to brothers is essential to selfhood in the modern life-world; it is a notion that must be taught.

Finally, there are words standing for intangibles. These enable the child to recognize its "mind-stuff": feelings, voices, images. Some of these are "just bad dreams," mother might say. "Everything is all right" despite them; the orderliness of things can be trusted. However, other mind-stuff must be attended to, for instance "conscience." This, which Freudians like to call the introjected voice of the Parent, is "real." "Good boys and girls always listen to their consciences." While, admittedly, this paints psychological development with an incredibly large brush, having once marked out for itself an internal compass of sorts, the child becomes capable of self-direction. With this comes the possibility of wanting to do and actually doing exactly what society prefers. At this point the child is endowed with the full complement of ego material.

Syntax and Self

The conversational accomplishment of ego involves more than learning to associate word-sounds with sensations. Grammar also plays a role.

Genie is the fictitious name of a 13-year-old girl admitted to a hospital after being isolated from human contact in a closet since infancy.[9] Although at first entirely unable to communicate verbally, within a year she had acquired an extensive vocabulary and the ability to construct two- and three-word declarative sentences such as "Father angry." "Father hit, big stick." "Hit, cry." Although Genie's semantic ability continued to expand, her grammatic capacity never developed beyond that of a normal 18- to 20-month-old child, even after five years of intense training. She could distinguish between plural and singular nouns, understand some prepositions, and use possessive pronouns accurately. She even learned to lie. She was never able to make negative statements beyond the primitive "Genie not have toy," and so forth; nor could she ask questions. (The interrogative mode often requires English-speakers to invert the word order of nouns and verbs, as in changing "The car is going" to "Is the car going?" Occasionally, it also involves using "wh" terms—"who," "what," "where," and so forth—at the beginning of sentences.) Instead, she constructed convoluted utterances like "I where is graham cracker on top shelf?"

Genie could neither summon people nor make requests. (Such operations often involve using what are known as subjunctive conditional verb forms like "would" and "could.") She was not able to use words in a performative way, that is, not only to describe things, but also to accomplish them, as in the sentences "Hello." "Thank you." "I will." Finally, although it seems a simple task, Genie was never able to use the subjective and objective terms for self, "I" and "me," correctly, and continued to confuse both with "you." As a result she found it difficult to engage in routine interactions with adults.

This point deserves closer examination. The following exchange recounts a real-life conversation between Jackie, an "educationally challenged" 10-year-old lad, and his volunteer instructor Mary.

Mary (shows Jackie a photograph of himself): "This is you."
Jackie (proudly agrees): "This is you."

Mary: "No, you (pointing to Jackie) are 'me.' "

Jackie (confused): "You are me."

Mary (points first to herself then to Jackie): "No, I am 'me.' *You* are 'you.' "

Jackie (thoroughly bewildered, carefully repeats what Mary says, pointing like Mary first to *himself*): "You are you." (And now points to Mary): "And I am me."

Mary (frustrated, tries a new tack): "No, Jackie is 'me' and 'I' am Mary."

Jackie (now with utmost concentration, mimics Mary): "Jackie is me and I am Mary."

Mary (points to Jackie): "No, 'you' are Jackie; 'I' am Mary. Jackie is 'I' *and* Jackie is 'me.' "

Jackie (dissolves in tears).

Sympathetically, we ask, how can three different pronouns "I," "me," and "you" not only apply to the same thing simultaneously, but equally to something entirely different?[10] It is this kind of grammatical discrimination that Genie was never able to master. As a consequence, she did not have a fully developed sense of self, an awareness of herself as a subject that can be an object to itself.

Genie was not retarded according to spatial and perspective tests. Furthermore, after five years her semantic lexicon was, to quote the examining psychologists, "extraordinarily large." She could sew, iron, draw both things and thoughts, and loved classical music. Brain scans revealed what was amiss: Genie used only her right cortical hemisphere. Psychologists drew two conclusions from this. First, grammatic capacity appropriate for adult functioning appears to be a left-brain operation. Second, and tragically for Genie, this neurological function may only be actionable at a specific age. Once the window of grammatic opportunity shuts, the likelihood of its ever being learned diminishes.

THAT THING CALLED "ME"

I have a sense of my place in the life-world (an identity), feelings of worth (esteem), and an idea of how I seem to others (an image).

These are the fundamental components of that thing called "me." What is the phenomenological essence of each?

Self-Identity

In popular sociology people are commonly written as "actors" whose identities are contained in the "roles" scripted for them in the "theater of life." An analogous idea is expressed in the ancient Japanese concept of *asobase-kotoba* (play-language), the form of address used by Buddhist aristocrats to display their indifference to (the presumed illusory nature of) worldly affairs. "The polite form for 'you arrive in Tokyo' is, literally, 'you *play* arrival in Tokyo'; and for 'I hear that your father is dead,' 'I hear that your father has *played* dying.' "[11]

As intriguing as it is to picture life as a game, a play, or as something "staged," this is far from being phenomenologically faithful to everyday experience.[12] For while I occasionally do experience myself as a performer who feigns emotions in an elaborate masquerade, most of the time I sense myself and my feelings as eminently *real*. In other words, ordinarily I am not detached from the life-world, standing above it in an attitude of aloof indifference, but like a vibrant tapestry, I am *firmly woven into it*. Essential to this weaving I call myself are my "warp" (my past), my "woof" (my group affiliations), and my situated roles here and now.[13]

Presently, I am a guest at Bob's Christmas party and have on my "party face." However, my identity is not reducible to this mask. I also bring to the event a memory of myself built upon past experience. Part of this is how, last year, I naively asked, "What's that?" when a hand-rolled cigarette-like substance in a roach clip was passed around and I was revealed as one unfamiliar with marijuana. I also recall with embarrassment being greeted at the door by a stark-naked man painted day-glow red. (We were asked to dress like our favorite Christmas characters. His was supposedly a tree ornament.) In addition, I step through Bob's front door as a member of an age group, a gender group, a racial group, and a professional group, and so forth. All these elements, woven together, comprise my identity, not just the party person I am playing.

Unlike myself, professional thespians are "decontextualized."

They are not fully woven into the fantasy worlds they concoct. They may play murderers, vamps, or detectives with insight and sensitivity, but their personal biographies and memberships are piled on the dressing room floor with their street clothes. Of course, to act with "insight and sensitivity" presupposes a certain amount of life-experience. Professional actors consciously draw upon such material as they would any "resource." In other words, real actors objectify their roles, distance themselves from their performances, see themselves *as* actors. As for the rest of us, for the most part we "act out" our parts, so to say, nonreflectively. We are laden down with a past filled with memories of successes, humiliations, and setbacks. Our parents, friends, and colleagues imaginatively hover over our shoulders, monitoring everything we do. Our party behavior, work habits, and buying patterns are so intertwined with our memories of who we are and with our affiliative backgrounds that we are hardly aware of acting at all.

True, there are moments when I am acutely conscious of "feeding people 'lines,' " " 'rehearsing' what I'm going to say," and "dressing the 'part,' " that is, of being a player enacting a script. This occurs in anticipation of novel situations like job interviews or first dates, or when I commit a faux pas and things are momentarily thrown out of kilter. Precisely when my reliability "vanishes," as Heidegger might say, *then* I become visible and distinct to myself as an actor.[14] Ordinarily, however, I am "dissolved" in the life-world, as invisible to myself as you are to me.

To say it again, the dramaturgic metaphor elucidates self-identity for persons estranged from the ordinary life-world; it is less helpful in depicting the experience of those woven into it.

Memory

Because it is the very "warp" of my identity, some further comments on memory are appropriate. Memory is essentially the past-as-it-is-for-me, how I am conscious of it. Like lived-time generally, it is conversationally accomplished. That is, the past is not given in the stream of one-thing-after-another as such. Rather, it is "remembered" (in contrast to "dis-membered"), by means of words. Among other things, this implies that I may have more than one past. For as I acquire new vocabularies (Marxism in place of the Christianity of my youth, and then later, the rubric of New Age channeling), things once considered all-important may be displaced and forgotten; others, previously "repressed," may be recalled.

It should be obvious that this observation applies not only to private biography, but also to public history (the memory of our life together). There can be no single definitive history of a nation. There can be only histories, stories related from different positions in time and social space: that reflecting the standpoint of conqueror and that of victim, that of male and that of female, that of the rich and that of the poor, and so forth. The same can be said of a people's identity as a people. It can never be a unitary whole, but rather must reflect the respective senses of its citizens' pasts.

Considerable attention has been paid recently to individuals recalling how they were abused as children.[15] Making these recollections doubly poignant is that many of their parents fervently deny the accusations. The following psychiatric account is typical:

> A heartbroken 65-year-old father of three daughters talked with me about his middle daughter's recent accusation (this did not involve criminal or civil law but rather was a private medical consultation) of the most graphic sexual abuses of her when she was still in her baby crib. . . . After involving herself for about two years in an "incest-survivor" group run by . . . "counselors," she had been referred to a . . . feminist "counselor" who repeatedly hypnotized her, regressing her [to retrieve past traumas]. The "counselors" are not . . . listed in the telephone directory, yet run their operation and have input and output with abuse centers receiving referrals from the courts.[16]

This is not the place to adjudicate the truth of the daughter's claims (or the father's denials); but two points should be kept in mind. First, events that never occurred can be "recalled" during counseling by perfectly sincere persons, even without conscious coaching by their therapists or by "regressive hypnosis." Furthermore, things that actually did happen can be lost down memory holes. What this suggests is that although memories are "remembered" by linguistic glue, some are more faithful to past occurrences than others.[17] Regardless of how histories and biographies are reconstructed, something *did* happen after all.

These two caveats notwithstanding, patients (as amateur biographers) typically have financial, emotional, and temporal investments in their therapists; they closely attend to feedback received during office visits. As a result they occasionally find themselves provisioned inadvertently with lay versions of their therapists' viewpoints. With these they begin rebuilding their pasts.

For their part, therapists sometimes unwittingly betray their boredom and disgust with clients who are "in denial" or who are "resisting." Meanwhile, they avidly greet "breakthroughs" and "real insights" with smiles and sighs of relief. The clients' own rage and tears of cathartic relief lend further credence to their recollections. As their "blockages are cleared," they may become convinced of what never occurred or forgetful of what did. Accurately recalled or not, the clients' lived-pasts alter, and with this their sense of who they are now.

Self-Esteem

I do not just want to "feel good" physically; I want to feel good about *myself*. I want to maximize my sense of esteem. To borrow Ernest Becker's phrasing, I want to know that my existence in the world is important, meaningful, heroic.[18] Human beings, says Becker, do not merely desire to be with God; they want to *be* gods. Why this is so remains a matter of dispute. For his part, Becker claims it is due to the consciousness of impending death—not theoretical death, death-in-the-abstract, but awareness of my own personal demise.

Whatever the source of this craving, the irony is that for human beings to feel good about themselves they often must feel *bad* physically (or must inflict pain on others). Think of dieting and exercise, of delaying gratification of wants until after graduation or until one is safely ensconced in a career. Think of tattooing, scarring, and other forms of self-mutilation, our species' primordial high arts. Think of the suicidal rites of *seppuku* (hara-kiri = belly slitting) or *sati* (suttee). After all, if we truly yearn for deification, and gods are spirit-beings, then we are required to mortify, to kill the flesh that binds us to earth. To assuage anxieties concerning our ultimate insignificance in the cosmos, we pile human skulls around ourselves.

Thus, there is ritual *sati*, the faithful Hindu wife's voluntary burial with her husband's corpse or her immolation on his funeral pyre. The Sanskrit word comes from the noun *sat*, meaning truth or being. Prior to its being outlawed, for the upper-caste Hindu wife "to be" in the most complete sense sometimes required her physical annihilation.[19] There is also *seppuku*, a ceremonial privilege by which a samurai warrior who had lost face could visibly display the purity of his soul to an audience of peers (the stomach being the soul's house).[20] The way to resuscitate one's esteem was by killing the body in the most excruciating way. To guarantee that the celebrant would not bring shame upon himself and his family, an attendant armed with a long sword was delegated to behead him at the slightest expression of pain.

As described by Charles Horton Cooley's theory of the looking glass, the social psychology of self-esteem involves three steps: I imagine how I appear to you; I imagine your judgment or appraisal of my appearance; and I feel either self-mortification or pride.[21] In short, says Cooley, my self-regard is a direct function of the approval you grant me. Ponder the Hindu wife and the obedient samurai in light of this formula: the psychic enhancement of both requires that their physical destruction be publicly witnessed, acknowledged, celebrated, and mourned.

The word "approval" literally means to judge some one, act, or thing good (*ad* [to] + *probus* [good]). According to Josef Pieper, to affirm the goodness of some one or thing is tantamount to saying, "I love you (or it)." If this is true, then my sense of self-regard (self-love) is predicated in some fundamental way on the reception of love from you. By loving me you justify my existence, confer on me the right to be, and in so doing encourage my survival. *"L'amour est par excellence ce qui fait etre"* ("Love is the essence of 'making to be' ").[22] This should not just be taken figuratively. Over half a century ago, Rene Spitz demonstrated that infants raised by their imprisoned mothers under abject conditions suffered fewer illnesses and neuroses, and had a lower mortality rate, than those brought up in well-equipped, hygienically impeccable orphanages by professional nurses. The institutionalized children received plenty of "milk," says Pieper, but not enough "honey."[23]

Of course, my esteem at any one moment is not simply a reflection of your response to me now.[24] Self-esteem is rarely just situational. First of all, I have a memory, a treasury of past judgments that I can draw upon to validate your opinion of me in the present. Judgments contrary to what I already "know" to be true, positively or negatively, may be ignored as "inaccurate," or they may be simply misread. Research indicates that those with low esteem tend to interpret signals from others so as to have this attitude confirmed. Those with high esteem are to an extent insulated from disparagement by not attending to it. Human beings are wonderfully adept at protecting what George Herbert Mead calls their "most precious part," their selves.

However this may be, in the final analysis my esteem does rest on your approval. However, affirmation and respect are rarely conferred unconditionally. Instead, they are contingent upon my providing you with pleasing information. To be sure, in "true" love, so to say, you affirm me for myself, not merely for how I please you.[25] This point aside, what Cooley says still stands: to solicit your respect, I must prove my worthiness.

Self-Image

Such proofs come in two forms. There is first the information I verbally "give" you, what I relate to you about myself. Then there is the information I "give off" (and occasionally betray) nonverbally.[26] Of these, you typically pay closer heed to the second. This is because it is less under my control and therefore a more valid indicator of who I "really" am. Since I have intuited already how you prioritize information sources, I attempt to control what I give off by packaging myself in agreeable ways, by presenting a front to you. The front is the public expression of my self-image. (Of course, it almost goes without saying that crucial to successfully staging a front is that I do it "spontaneously" and "naturally," lest you see through it for the facade it is.) Erving Goffman has detailed the elements of any complete front.

First of all there is my appearance. This includes my physique, but more often my clothing style, fabric, and manufacturer's label, their newness, cleanliness, and color balance; my shoes (or lack thereof); my hair style and color; and above all, my facial features: whether I wear glasses, have a beard, or am painted—how and to what degree, and so forth.

Next is my manner, my kinesics or body language proper, how I hold myself and move: my hand gestures, gait, sitting posture, and "face work," as Goffman calls it. "The eyes are windows to the soul." Therefore, central to face work is eye movement—soulful glances, wide-eyed wonderment, eyelid-shielding coolness. Under the category of manner is included voicing—whether I speak shrilly, softly, or intensely. Finally, there is my rhetorical style. Will I "present" as a back-slapping good ole' boy, a carefully spoken professor, or a self-righteous preacher?

Then there is the setting, my strategic placement of scenic apparatuses to foster impressions: the types of furniture I surround myself with—books, tapes, and magazines calculatedly "strewn" so as to be seen by visitors; toilet paper quality and scent; the juxtaposing of toilet to bath (if any), and their sizes, tints, and shapes; wall and floor coverings—their texture, color, and ply; the contents of my tool chest, my kitchen utensils, and my electronic gadgetry. Above all is my vehicular extension: whether it is a pinstriped, gun-racked, big-wheeled Ford Bronco or a grey-bodied, tinted-windowed, white-tired Cadillac, and so forth. Human beings not only do art, Goffman concludes, we *are* art. We are first of all our own creations.

Despite my best efforts (sometimes precisely because I am trying *too* hard), cracks may appear in my front. A single mother on her first date in years spends anxious hours before the mirror, primping. Later that evening, strolling into a grocery store with the young man to purchase some bottled refreshment, she glances down in horror to see she has on one red and one green shoe. Gail has fostered the impression of being a sophisticate. Soon after downing some bourbon, however, she slips while descending the stage steps, and lands on the dance floor, legs askew, formal dress around her waist, red faced. At a televised, formal dinner the president of the United States vomits into the lap of his foreign host. A French Catholic cardinal is found dead of a heart attack in the apartment of a well-heeled prostitute.

Perhaps I tried to forewarn you of the impending misplay in order to soften its damage: "I don't want to hurt anyone's feelings (that is, I am really a decent chap), but . . ."; "Some of my best friends are Indians (Jews, black people) thus I'm not really a racist, but . . ."; "I haven't done this in a long time (so even if I screw up now, that does not mean I am not really good at it)." These are known as disclaimers; through them I "disown" the untoward act I am at risk of committing.

If my warnings have failed to prepare you ahead of time (and assuming the inconsistency is too glaring to ignore), you will likely bring me to task for it. The microcosm we jointly fashioned wherein I became a particular thing to you (and you, to me) has been shattered. My responsibility is to renominize the situation by offering "motives," good reasons, for what has happened: excuses or justifications.[27] In the event you refuse to "buy" my account, I may have to go further: apologizing, perhaps even making reparations—giving you flowers or favors, or paying you court-assessed damages. Once you have forgiven my betrayal, however, the onus is on me once again, this time to endorse it with my thanks. By these simple gestures your investment in the things of the world (namely, me) is protected.[28]

In excusing myself, I acknowledge the seriousness of my transgression, but insist that I am not responsible for it.[29] This is because allegedly it was beyond my control (from *ex* [outside] + cause): "It was in my genes." "I had no choice, he had a gun." "I was temporarily insane." or "I was abused as a child." Justifications are different. Here, I accept responsibility for what was done, but try to convince you that it was all right.[30] Either no actual harm was done, or, if it was, you deserved it, or even if you didn't, I was following a higher law: "I am essentially a peace lover, but I bombed this office to strike against Zionist Occupation Government!" or "I know 'Thou shalt not kill,' but I took the doctor's life to save unborn children!" It is an increasingly familiar and discomfiting experience for judges to hear bowdlerized versions of Marxism, psychiatry, biology, and both liberal and conservative social philosophy invoked by wrong-doers to excuse or justify their crimes. Today, as one commentator has noted, "everyone is a 'victim.' "[31]

CONCLUSION

As Genie and Jackie discovered to their misfortune, self is paradoxical indeed. For it is that singular thing in the life-world that can be an object to itself, simultaneously an "I" and a "me," both a subject *and* an object.

"Me" is my lived-self. It has a definite identity, a measure of worth, and is discernible to others. In contrast, "I" is not a thing at all. It is "nothing." It is that that is in the dark about myself. Insofar as what lurks in darkness is potentially dangerous, it is entirely reasonable that Freud pictured it as an Id (an It), a welter of world-destroying energy. Nonetheless, such a portrayal betrays his psychology as the projection of a world-weary, end-of-century pessimist. After all, we might just as truly predicate "I," as have many American liberals (Ernest Becker and George Herbert Mead among them), that "I" is the boundless source of individual freedom, uniqueness, and creativity. The point is that *any* definitive characterization of "I" is an exercise in futility. This is not to say that we can therefore ignore whatever is posited of "I." Doctrines of human essence harbor political implications. Pessimistic psychologies call for restraint and discipline, if not granted voluntarily they will be imposed by force. Liberalism advocates policies that protect and enlarge individual rights.

However this may be, "I" is, and forever shall remain, the *mysterious* personal ground of my being-in-the-world. It is a gift. "Me," in contrast, is my "personhood" (*persona*), my mask(s), the wrappings in which this gift comes. As we have seen, this package emerges out of conversation, and is twined and knotted with words. As the self's veil, "me" simultaneously reveals and conceals. It discloses the being of "I" precisely as it hides from me what "it" is. "I" is the mythical hide-behind, the creature who by positioning tree trunks between itself and the viewer is always *"invisibly* there." "Me" (the trunk) is that without which the hide-behind could not be disclosed.

NOTES

1. Erich Neumann, *The Origins and History of Consciousness* (Princeton, NJ: Princeton University Press, 1973 [1954]).

2. Thomas N. Tentler, *Sin and Confession on the Eve of the Reformation* (Princeton, NJ: Princeton University Press, 1977).

3. Bernard Haring, "The Phenomenology of the Scrupulous Conscience," in *The Law of Christ*, ed. Bernard Haring (Cork, Ireland: Mercier Press, 1963), pp. 157–69.

4. Emile Durkheim, *The Division of Labor in Society*, trans. George Simpson (New York: Free Press, 1964 [1893]).

5. Leonard Carmichael, "The Early Growth of Language Capacity in the Individual," in *New Directions in the Study of Language*, ed. Eric Lenneberg (Cambridge, MA: Massachusetts Institute of Technology, 1966), pp. 1–22.

6. John Hewitt, *Self & Society*, 5th ed. (Boston: Allyn and Bacon, 1991), pp. 110–12.

7. Bruno Bettelheim, *Symbolic Wounds* (New York: Collier Books, 1954), pp. 52–53, 138–41, 143–44.

8. Suzanne Bunkers, *In Search of Susanna* (Iowa City: University of Iowa Press, 1996), pp. 191–92. My emphasis.

9. Susan Curtiss, *Genie: A Psycholinguistic Study of a Modern Day "Wild-Child"* (New York: Academic Press, 1977).

10. This paradox has occupied the attention of semioticians, most notably Emile Beniveste. His conclusion is that "I" and "you" have no reference to an organic reality at all, but merely to different "sites" in a conversation. Some semioticians have taken this to mean that human subjectivity in-itself is nothing but a linguistic event. See Katja Silverman, *The Subject of Semiotics* (New York: Oxford University Press, 1983), pp. 43–46, 126–30.

11. Johann Huizinga, *Homo Ludens*, trans. R.F.C. Hull (London: Routledge & Kegan Paul, 1949), p. 5.

12. James Ostrow, "Spontaneous Involvement and Social Life," *Sociological Perspectives* 39 (Fall 1996): 341–51.

13. Hewitt, *Self & Society*, pp. 120–24.

14. Martin Heidegger, *Being and Time*, trans. John Macquarri and Edward Robinson (New York: Harper and Row, 1962), pp. 126–27, 164.

15. Lawrence Wright, *Remembering Satan* (New York: Alfred A. Knopf, 1994).

16. G. Christian Harris, M.D., "Abusing the Abuser—I'm Only Trying to Help You" (Paper presented at the Seventh Annual Symposium of the American College of Forensic Psychiatry, San Diego, CA, 31 March 1989), p. 9. Harris writes that "two interviews with the 25-year old daughter convinced me of her borderline psychotic pathology."

17. Elizabeth Loftus, *Witness for the Defense* (New York: St. Martin's Press, 1991).

18. Ernest Becker, *Angel in Armor* (New York: Free Press, 1969). For his classic study, see Becker, *The Denial of Death* (New York: Free Press, 1973). For a critique of this idea, see John Hewitt, *The Myth of Self-Esteem* (New York: St. Martin's Press, 1998).

19. Joseph Campbell, *The Masks of God* (New York: Viking Press, Inc., 1970), 2: 62–67.

20. Jack Seward, *Hara-Kiri: Japanese Ritual Suicide* (Rutland, VT: Charles E. Tuttle Co., 1968).

21. Charles Horton Cooley, *Human Nature and Social Order* (New York: Charles Scribner's Sons, 1902), p. 152.

22. Maurice Blondel, quoted in Josef Pieper, *About Love*, trans. Richard Winston and Clara Winston (Chicago: Franciscan Herald Press, 1974), p. 23. See also pp. 18–25.

23. Ibid., p. 28.

24. Hewitt, *Self & Society*, pp. 139–41.

25. On the other hand, contrary to the admonition implied in the title *I'm OK, You're OK*, complete love never affirms everything about the other, including his or her vices, for being less than he or she might be. Rather, it scolds, chastens, warns, and nags. See Thomas Harris, *I'm OK, You're OK* (New York: Harper and Row, 1969).

26. Erving Goffman, *The Presentation of Self in Everyday Life* (Garden City, NY: Doubleday-Anchor, 1959), pp. 22–30.

27. For the classic analysis of the rhetoric of motives, see C. Wright Mills, "Situated Actions and the Vocabulary of Motives," *American Sociological Review* 5 (December 1940): 904–13. For an elaboration, see C. Wright Mills and Hans Gerth, *Character and Social Structure* (New York: Harcourt, Brace and World, 1953), pp. 112–29.

28. Erving Goffman, *Interaction Ritual* (Garden City, NY: Doubleday-Anchor, 1967), pp. 97–112.

29. For disclaimers, see Hewitt, *Self & Society*, pp. 187–88, and John Hewitt and Randall Stokes, "Disclaimers," *American Sociological Review* 40 (February 1975): 1–11. For justifications and excuses, see Hewitt, *Self & Society*, pp. 188–90, and Marvin Scott and Stanford Lyman, "Accounts," *American Sociological Review* 33 (December 1968): 46–62.

30. Gresham Sykes, "Techniques of Neutralization, a Theory of Delinquency," *American Sociological Review* 22 (December 1957): 664–70.

31. Charles Sykes, *Nation of Victims: The Decay of American Character* (New York: St. Martin's Press, 1992).

5

YOU

"Me" cannot be posed as an object of experience without that to which it is *op*posed, "you." You are the person to whom I attend most closely. This is because I need you, if not for physical care then for emotional succor, particularly affirmation. As Jean-Paul Sartre shows in *No Exit*, without your being-there for me I begin to doubt my own substantiality. You are my "former," Emmanuel Levinas agrees, my prior. You teach me who and what I am by your words and gestures. My debt to you is therefore limitless.[1] For you to serve as my teacher I must first understand your words and gestures. I must have a grasp of your mind. "When he says I'm 'stunning,' does he really mean it, or is he just being nice?" "Was that comment—'you're a great shot'—meant sincerely, or was it sarcasm?" "Is Peter's failure to acknowledge my smiling wave intended as an insult, or didn't he see me?" Tragic, sometimes deadly, consequences result from misunderstanding one another's expressions.

How, then, is knowledge of others' minds possible? How do I know you, and you me? This chapter presents two answers to this question. One is the orthodox view proffered by mainline symbolic interactionists. The competing view is expounded, among others, by Max Scheler and Maurice Merleau-Ponty.

The orthodox account comes in several variations, each a bit more sophisticated.[2] The simplest is analogy theory; the most well-known, role-taking theory; and the most elaborate, the theory of "apperceptive transference" or projection. Despite their differences all three notions insist that knowledge of others emerges from a quasi-rational process. Here, I call it empathy.

The advocates of heterodoxy dispute the claim that cognizance of other minds is fundamentally rational. Instead, they insist that it is sympathetic and emotionally based. We know other people not through our heads, at least not exclusively, but by our hearts.[3]

EMPATHY

Paula and Ed are on their first date. For the encounter to be reasonably satisfying, both must have some knowledge of why the other is acting as he or she is. Why, asks Paula, is Ed taking me for dinner to the expensive Casa del Rio instead of to a more moderately priced place? Why to this movie and not to another? Why is he picking me up in this nice car instead of that rather beat-up truck I saw him driving yesterday? Ed, meanwhile, is undertaking an analogous inquiry. Why did Paula want me to meet her at the bus stop on Poplar Avenue instead of at home? To call her at this time and not another? Why is she dressed in this way? Given the complexity of even these routine inquiries, it is a wonder that human beings socialize effectively at all. That we do, raises the question, how?

Orthodoxy explains mutuality this way. Ed and Paula have a good idea of their own purposes in doing things, and each has access to the other's movements and utterances. However, they cannot see directly into one another's minds. Hence, they do the next best thing: they imaginatively put themselves in the place of the other. They "take the role of the other," to use George Herbert Mead's phrase, and infer the other's intentions by reasoning this way: were I, says Paula to herself, to take a first date to dinner at a place like this, then to a movie like that, in a fine automobile, then this is what *I* would mean by doing so. Ed does the same. In Alfred Schutz's words, "I attribute to alter the same perspective which I should have if I were not 'here' but 'there' [in alter's position]."[4]

In attempting to understand each other, both Paula and Ed argue from analogy using their own experience as a primary premise. To say it technically, insofar as neither Ed nor Paula can literally place himself or herself in the other's head, each "transfers" his or her own mentality onto the other, saying that if *I* were to do such and such, this is what *I* would mean by doing so. Understood this way, empathy is not a passive "opening up" to others, at least not this alone; it is an active attribution, a "superimposition" of my intentionality onto you; "an objectification of myself in an object distinct from myself."[5]

The possibility of empathetic projection rests on the assumption that the mental life of the other person, at least as far as it relates to his or her behavior, corresponds to the knower's own. Without this assumption, their actions would "remain nothing but a meaningless and incoherent chaos."[6] This is why Simmel can claim that "whoever has never loved will never understand love or the lover; someone with a passionate disposition will never understand one who is apathetic. The weakling will never understand the hero, nor will the hero ever understand the weakling."[7]

To demonstrate the logic of empathy, I have reconstructed Paula's mental gymnastics syllogistically. The reader is encouraged to do the same with Ed.

Major premise$_1$: If I were to take a first date to an expensive restaurant, then I would be trying to impress her.

Major premise$_2$: Edward's mental life, as it concerns his behavior, is similar to my own.

Minor premise: On our first date, Edward takes me to the tony restaurant, Casa del Rio.

Therefore: Edward is trying to impress me.

Given this conclusion, Paula now has a better idea of how to respond to Ed's gesture, for example, by effusively displaying appreciation. It should be emphasized, however, that Paula's conclusion is a hypothesis only. When she acts on it, the hypothesis's truth is "tested" by Ed's response to her appreciation. If he ignores her "thank you" or seems confused by her enthusiasm, then one of three things is wrong: Ed's "mental life" does not correspond to Paula's own, after all (a frequent occurrence among people of the opposite gender); her way of displaying appreciation is some-how inappropriate; Paula is naive about *her own* motives; or per-haps all three. Assuming Paula and Ed wish to sustain their relationship they will continue their efforts at imaginative role-taking until their respective hypotheses concerning one another's mind are confirmed.

Stages in Role-Taking Ability

Human beings have the genetic capacity to empathize with oth-ers, but it is a potential that requires cultivation and refinement before they are capable of socializing like Paula and Ed. Mead outlines the stages through which people pass in acquiring this skill: play, games, and the generalized other.[8] Subsequent com-mentators would add a prior stage, preplay, referring to the infant's random exploration of its surroundings. The generalized other is discussed in the next chapter.

Play

"Words imply deeds," says John Hewitt.[9] The meaning of "bad man" is one who should be avoided; "God's house," where one wears her pretty pink dress and black pumps, and sits solemnly when brother tries to make her laugh; "mamma," one to whom I am to go when in tears. According to Mead, the deedlike meanings of social terms are learned through "play." The child plays char-acters significant in its life by imaginatively reenacting their roles. The child learns the meaning of "mother," for example, by clum-sily, endearingly aping what it sees its mother do: caring for baby, setting the table, and washing clothes; mimicking mother's moods, her tone of voice, the way she holds her body and works her face, the way she greets daddy as he comes through the door. Parents occasionally are embarrassed by what their children betray about themselves as parents through play-acting.

The child playfully takes the roles of fireman, dentist, and teacher—talking, dressing, and emoting as it imagines they do. By this, its empathetic skills are honed. It slowly learns to be in the world, as Alfred Schutz might say, as if the child "were not 'here' but 'there' " in the fireman's, dentist's, or teacher's position.

Crucial to play is the child seeing and thinking about *itself* as it imagines these others do, with fondness or irritation, with joy or revulsion. This is the "looking glass self" alluded to in the last chapter: the idea that children judge themselves as others do, and by this acquire varying degrees of esteem.

Games

Games take the process one step further. Here the child organizes the roles of several others simultaneously into a gestalt, an abstract whole, and then imaginatively puts itself in the place of that whole. Mead uses baseball as an example. To play baseball, batters must not only be able to coordinate their eyes with hand and trunk motions; they also must be able to assume the separate roles of catcher, first baseman, and pitcher toward themselves as batters. Above all, they must be able to constitute all three positions into an opposing "team" with a general perspective toward events on the field, particularly toward the batter. An opposing team, after all, is not merely the sum of its players. It is a coordinated entity, a *sui generis*, having the goal of keeping the batter off base. It is this entity the child must grasp if it is to play the *game* of baseball, as opposed to merely hitting, throwing, and catching.

This is analogous to being a functioning member of society. Socially adept adults are more than just skilled performers of separate roles. They have a sense of being members of a bounded reality, "America," "Israel," or "China," distinguishable by its own values and destiny: a whole greater than the sum of its parts. Adults are able to take the (imagined) attitude of this unity toward themselves, consider what "they" think about him or her, and govern themselves accordingly. In this respect, games are not just idle recreations; they are training grounds for participation in "real" life.

Parties

The acquisition of role-taking ability does not end in childhood. Simmel writes of adult party-going as an opportunity to refine one's empathetic skills.[10] In lunching with others, drinking together, jointly celebrating birthdays and the like, party-goers playfully rehearse for the serious affairs of business and politics. They cast off their wealth for a short time, along with their worldly burdens, their fame, and their demerits. They then proceed to pleasure themselves in the simple act of being sociable, amiable, courteous, cordial, and coquettish. The heart and core of party-life is artful conversation, rapid word-play: deftly reading one another's signs, and responding to them with discretion, tact, and sensitivity. Having had their role-taking skills reinvigorated, party-goers are prepared to step back into the workaday world.

CRITICIZING ORTHODOXY

Max Scheler criticizes the theory of empathetic understanding on both logical and empirical grounds.[11]

Logical Problems

To begin with Scheler acknowledges that the theory of empathy does describe something familiar. We do occasionally argue from analogy in determining others' intentions and internal states. Furthermore, historians, ethnographers, and clinical psychologists do the same in attempting to grasp the actions of long-deceased historical figures, the customs and beliefs of alien peoples, and their patients' fantasies and dreams.[12] Even so, empathy is not sufficient to explain knowledge of others' minds, says Scheler. This is because it already presupposes such knowledge.

While empathy describes how we know the content of others' minds, says Scheler, it begs the question of how we know others *have* minds in the first place. Not every movement provokes empathy. Trains and cars move, but we do not try to understand them; rivers flow, and at least ordinarily we do not seek to know their minds. On the contrary, we seek to comprehend the intentions only of those things already attributed with subjectivity, specifically, human beings. To be sure, some people inhabit enchanted life-worlds wherein plants, water, and even rocks are animated. The question remains: how do we know this to be the case? Empathy theory presupposes such knowledge; but it is unable to account for how it comes to be.

Scheler's second objection is that the theory of empathetic understanding assumes that we use our observations of others' movements to infer their mental states by glimpsing a parallel between their movements and our own. However, what we see of others' bodily movements by no means corresponds to what we experience of our own. What I sense *kinesthetically* when I move my own legs is not the same as what I *perceive* optically in your legs moving. What (if anything) I sense of myself in smiling at you is by no means identical to what I see when you smile at me. Thus, there is little basis for inferring your mental state from an examination of my own. On the contrary, says Scheler, I must already have some knowledge of your internal state before empathy can proceed. Empathy may account for what occurs after having acquired this knowledge; but it does not reveal from where it comes.

Third, unless the existence of other minds is already presupposed, the only inference logically permitted me on the basis of my observations of your movements is not the content of your mind, but that *my mind* is also "there" in your body. Indeed, this is what Alfred Schutz seems to imply when he asserts that while empathizing, the knower is "no longer 'here' but 'there' in the other's place." This leads to perhaps the gravest weakness of orthodoxy, namely, that if it is true, then empathizers are in essence conversing not with each other, *but with their own projections*. Because each infers the other's intentions only after reflecting on what it would mean to himself or herself were he or she to act this way, then there can be no true meeting of minds. Mutual understanding in any but a superficial sense is logically precluded. Each is doomed forever to solipsistic isolation. While some might find this acceptable, Scheler does not.

Empirical Problems

Infants and even animals, says Scheler, can "read" our expressions, respond to coos, hugs, frowns, and finger shakings. Nevertheless, we would be reluctant to insist that this is because they engage in the kind of reasoning attributed to Ed and Paula. If this is true of infants and animals, the same must be true of adults. There are no grounds for believing that our powers of understanding are any less than those of babies or dogs. Furthermore, we sometimes claim to be able to understand parakeets, horses, and even wild animals on the basis of *their* expressions. This is hardly because we assume (as in the second major premise in the syllogism) that their mental life corresponds to our own.

In the second place, human beings are capable of understanding others' feelings even if they have not had such feelings themselves. Simmel's claim that those who have never loved can never understand the lover is simply not true. I need not ever to have been tortured to comprehend the screams of its victims, nor ever to have lost a child to know the joy of a mother having recovered her's. The case of children who, while minimally experienced, seem able to grasp others' emotional states and moods, is instructive. They are not prisoners of their pasts. Even Simmel admits that a historian need never have been Caesar to understand Caesar. Given his commitment to empathy theory, however, he cannot say how this is possible.

The Assumptions of Empathy Theory Reexamined

Although the orthodox view has several variations, all of them make the same two assumptions and from them draw the same conclusion: (1) the knower at the outset has full knowledge of its own mental contents, its own thoughts, intentions, and meanings of why it acts as it does, and (2) the only other things directly available to the knower are "coats and hats passing by," not intentionally acting persons. Therefore, the knower's belief that others have minds (and what those are) is entirely derivative. In other words, you are in effect nothing but an object constituted by me, an "objectification of my self in an object separate from myself." You are my own projection, my own project. I have made you what you are, at least what you are for me.

Scheler objects to these suppositions, saying that together they exaggerate the difficulty of knowing others while underestimating the difficulty of knowing ourselves.

First, contrary to popular opinion, private experience is *not* the first thing given us as human beings, either historically or psychologically. What is first given us is sensation, period. Only after children have acquired language—first names, personal pronouns, and possession terms like "my" and "mine"—are they positioned to sculpt themselves out of this sensory confusion. Only then are they capable of identifying the stream of sensation with distinct individuals, me and you. Far from being primary, then, it is "me" and *its* experiences that are secondary and derivative.

Second, it is not true that I am only capable of perceiving your outward movements. Instead, I seem to be in direct contact with your feelings through these movements. I know your joy through your laughter; feel your sorrow and pain in witnessing your tears; sense shame in your blush; find love in your affectionate gaze. The laughter, the tears, the blushes, and the tender glances are not just signs representing inner meanings, they *are* the very meanings they convey. Again, I do not just observe your eyes fixed on a particular object (me), *I see you looking at me.* I detect an intention *in* your very gaze. I do not simply observe the flush of blood in your cheeks. After all, this could have many causes: a red light casting its hue on your face, debauchery, sunburn, overexertion. Instead, I see *you blushing.*

Third, the conclusion that you are merely a product of my own labor, that I "make you" by attributing you with a mentality analogous to my own is, to use Scheler's phrase, the height of egocentrism. It reflects a bias of modern thought that asserts that ultimately everything revolves around the Transcendent Ego, Me. Egocentrism cripples our capacity to recognize the independent ontology of other living things and, related to this, their ultimate worth apart from their utility for me.

Given these considerations, Scheler is driven to locate human mutuality in a different place, in a feeling, one he calls sympathy. Knowledge of others, he says, arises not from logical inferences from the ego's standpoint, but from a feeling-with others. Feeling is the fundamental basis of mutuality, not thinking. We are connected to each other not through our heads alone, not even most importantly in this way, but through our hearts.

SYMPATHY

Paula and Ed can and do "read" one another's gestures, clothing, and utterances. They "decode" one another's meanings so as to be able to react effectively to them. Normally they do this only after having achieved some distance from the encounter: when one or the other has gone to the lavatory, for example, or out to the car, or when they are back in their respective apartments, mulling over the evening's events. At that point each assumes the attitude of an amateur scientist, entertaining various hypotheses concerning the other's behaviors as "texts." Each reflects, perhaps with horror and anxiety, on the possible "misreadings" the other might have made of himself or herself based on those texts: "I talked too much, I just know he'll think I'm pushy." "Why did I have to make that stupid comment about fat people? She'll probably think I'm an insensitive brute." "I'm so clumsy, I made an ass out of myself when we danced."

Typically such analyses occur only later. During the course of the date itself, Paula and Ed *undergo* each other's physicality, his or her respective voicings, odors, appearances, gazes, and touches. In this condition, they are *immediately* repelled, turned on, put at ease, or fascinated by one another. That is, they respond to each other without their rational, hypothesizing minds fully engaged. Scheler encompasses prereflective, nonmediated mutual sensitivity under the general category of sympathy.

Following their date, Paula and Ed go over the evening, examining each other (and themselves from the other's standpoint) as objects. Here, the empathetic process described earlier holds true. During the course of the date itself, however, each relates to the other sympathetically, not as subject to object, but as subject to subject. Scheler encompasses true intersubjectivity under the category "We." His French counterpart, Maurice Merleau-Ponty, would later write of it as the natural condition of our "irreducible interwoven-ness."[13] Both Scheler and Merleau-Ponty agree with Martin Heidegger that conversation is never simply the transmission of messages from the interior of one person to the interior of another. Rather, discourse makes possible their conscious taking hold of, their explicit appropriation of an *already* shared world.[14]

Clarifications

"Mistaken" Sympathy

That I occasionally sympathize incorrectly, as it were, does not refute the fact of our fundamental interconnectedness, Scheler insists. True, I may have received the wrong impression from your tears, laughter, or arched eyebrows, and responded in ways I now regret. For instance, Helen's throat constricted and her sinuses filled when the mother whom she later learned had murdered her own child sobbingly beseeched the TV audience for its safe return. Helen's original sympathetic response was not to her reflective (mis)understanding of the mother's weeping. It was to the tears themselves in the immediacy of the moment. True, with sophistication gained through humiliating revelations of sympathetic naiveté Helen may yet learn to control her disposition to feel-with others too readily. This, however, merely demonstrates that the human capacity to sympathize can be, and often is, superseded by the acquisition of reflective empathetic skills.

The Lived-Body

The question still remains: how exactly can Helen sense sadness and terror in the mother's distraught face, or myself love in your affectionate gaze, and so forth?[15] Merleau-Ponty answers this with his notion of the "lived-body," a concept that conjoins mind-stuff to outward movement.

The lived-body is "consciousness made flesh," body consciousness, the experience of my own corporeality. According to Merleau-Ponty, phenomenologically speaking mind and body are really opposite sides of the same coin. Outward movements are not just "signs" of internal states, "codes" to be read or "deciphered" empathetically. Instead, *physicality already resonates with significance; gestures, with the meanings they express.*

When I encounter a strange person on a dark, abandoned street, "the stranger is not *conceived of* as frightening; he *is* frightening—that is just what his presence is, irreducibly, at this fearful moment."[16] Later, behind my locked apartment door, trying to give my sensations words, I may put myself imaginatively in the stranger's shoes to interpret his being on the street at that hour. However, during the incident itself, my heart begins pounding and my breathing gasps immediately at the sight of his spectral form looming from the shadows.

Again, let us revisit Paula and Ed. Their "insides and outsides are wholly inseparable"; their internal feelings and behaviors are merely opposing surfaces of the same body-sense. Therefore, each can suffer the other's physicality directly without having consciously to interpret what is happening.

Contra Schutz

In fairness to empathy theory, it should be mentioned that Alfred Schutz, for one, would concur with Merleau-Ponty that we do not constantly have to figure out how to categorize people on the basis of the cues they provide before being able to socialize with them. This would render the rapid-fire character of everydayness impossible. On the contrary, we are able to "tune in" to each other nonreflectively and immediately. Schutz's account of what transpires on such occasions is far from what Merleau-Ponty has in mind.

According to Schutz, nonreflective mutuality is possible because the meanings of most cues have already been pregiven.[17] Since this is true, our responses to them can be unthinking, automatic. Picture the American car driver's disposition to assume the right lane even when there is no oncoming traffic. The driver does not have to be reminded each time he takes the wheel which lane is correct. All the same, lane assignments are not given in the nature of street travel itself. They are allotted by convention. Having been habituated to this convention, the driver can now proceed without thought.

Contrast this to Merleau-Ponty. For Merleau-Ponty our engagement with one another is nonreflective not because it is habitual, but because it is sympathetic, feeling based. It is grounded in a *pre*conceptual, *pre*definitional, intuitive sensitivity we have to each other's bodily presence. Two phrases Merleau-Ponty employs to characterize this state are "mutual sensitivity without significance" and "coherency without concept." Later, he would call it the state of having a "common flesh." Prior to and beneath our objective relating, he says, we are of the same body. Mutuality is possible because we *already* occupy a common home.

In saying this, Merleau-Ponty is self-consciously addressing a theme in existentialism to be discussed in chapter 8, homelessness. Modern ego experiences itself as arbitrarily thrown into the cosmos, alone. What Merleau-Ponty and Scheler have shown is that this experience is a consequence of forgetfulness. Specifically, in its frantic quest for distinction, ego has forgotten its original domicile, the common flesh out of which it emerged, the We. Merleau-Ponty and Scheler have prepared a path back home.

CONCLUSION

"Sympathy" means feeling-with others; "empathy," rationally understanding them. Both are pivotal for interaction, but neither necessarily implies the other. To feel compassion for victims of the Holocaust, I must first grasp how they experienced death camp routines. Imaginatively putting myself in their place does not necessarily evoke sympathy. It can also inspire mirth, gloating, or indifference.

By the same token, sympathy occasionally can occur without empathy. Consider a run on the arena entrances by general admission ticket holders to a rock concert. Each gate-crasher is visited by the same dread of being left behind when the crowd lurches forward, and so pushes that much more furiously to get in front. Here, we might say, each individual is "infected" by the crowd's behavior; the result is disaster.

Scheler considers mass contagions and hypnotic suggestion to be examples of "pathological sympathy"—pathological because those who are emotionally affected are unconscious of the actual sources of their feelings. Bona fide fellow-feeling, he says, occurs only when others' feelings are given to us as having a unique reality and a value equal to our own. In the highest form of sympathy, you are neither merged with me, nor do I consider your feelings any less important than my own. Instead, each of us maintains our individual integrity. Scheler calls this human love.[18]

Which is more fruitful in explaining knowledge of other minds, sympathy or empathy? While both are important, empathy is possible only after ego and alter have been parceled out from the continuum of sensation. Furthermore, empathy requires that ego be able to objectify alter's actions from its own (ego's) viewpoint. These preconditions can be met only after considerable psychological development. Therefore, empathy cannot be considered the originary basis for knowing other minds. Instead, this can only be found in a preconceptual source, namely, in our preobjective, preanalytical, natural sensitivity to others. The originary basis for knowing other minds, in other words, must have something to do with sympathy.

NOTES

1. Emmanuel Levinas, *Otherwise Than Being*, trans. Alphonso Lingus (The Hague: Martinus Nijhoff, 1981).
2. For the role-taking version of empathetic understanding, see Ralph

H. Turner, "Role-Taking, Role-Standpoint, and Reference Group Behavior," *American Journal of Sociology* 61 (1956): 316–28. For the notion of empathetic projection, see Georg Simmel, *The Problems of the Philosophy of History: An Epistemological Essay*, trans. Guy Oakes (New York: Free Press, 1977). Although Simmel addresses the discipline of history, it is clear that his comments also apply to routine social interaction. Edith Stein has written a somewhat obscure analysis, *On the Nature of Empathy*, trans. Waltraut Stein (The Hague: Martinus Nijhoff, 1964). It is based on the theory of analogy developed by her mentor, Edmund Husserl, *Cartesian Meditations*, trans. Dorian Cairns (The Hague: Martinus Nijhoff, 1977), pp. 108–11.

3. For the classic presentation of the heterodox view, see Max Scheler, *The Nature of Sympathy*, trans. Peter Heath, intro. Werner Stark (London: Routledge & Kegan Paul, 1958). Excerpts from this book may also be found in Max Scheler, *On Feeling, Knowing, and Valuing*, ed. and intro. Harold J. Bershady (Chicago: University of Chicago Press, 1992), pp. 49–81. A summary of Scheler's position is found in Alfred Schutz, "Scheler's Theory of Intersubjectivity," in *Collected Papers*, ed. and intro. Maurice Natanson (The Hague: Martinus Nijhoff, 1973), 1:156–79.

4. Schutz, *Collected Papers*, 1:178.

5. These assertions are paraphrased from Simmel and Stein, respectively.

6. Simmel, *The Problems of the Philosophy of History*, p. 45.

7. Ibid., p. 65.

8. George Herbert Mead, *Mind, Self and Society*, ed. Charles W. Morris (Chicago: University of Chicago Press, 1934), pp. 135–73.

9. John Hewitt, *Self & Society*, 5th ed. (Boston: Allyn and Bacon, 1991 [1976]), pp. 113–14.

10. Georg Simmel, "Sociability," in *The Sociology of Georg Simmel*, trans. and ed. Kurt H. Wolff (New York: Free Press, 1964), pp. 40–57.

11. Scheler, *The Nature of Sympathy*, pp. 37–50, 213–64.

12. Role-taking as a research technique is known in sociology as *verstehen*, "empathetic understanding." *Verstehen* literally means standing in the position of one's opposite. For the classic discussion of the place of *verstehen* in sociology, see Max Weber, *The Theory of Social and Economic Organization*, trans. and intro. Talcott Parsons (New York: Free Press, 1947), pp. 87–100.

13. Merleau-Ponty's classic statement is found in his *Phenomenology of Perception*, trans. C. Smith (Atlantic Highlands, NJ: Humanities Press, 1962). For a readable if challenging introduction to Merleau-Ponty, see James Ostrow, *Social Sensitivity* (Albany: State University of New York Press, 1990).

14. Martin Heidegger, *Being and Time*, trans. John Macquarri and Edward Robinson (New York: Harper and Row, 1962), p. 205.

15. It has been said that in postulating We as the primary experience, Scheler has lost sight of individuality altogether, and with it true *intersubjectivity* in the sense of mutuality between independent persons. If true, this means that Scheler is just as incapable of accounting for mutual understanding as are the advocates of empathy theory, but for the opposite reason.

16. Ostrow, *Social Sensitivity*, p. 2. For an excellent example, see pp. 62–66.

17. Schutz, *Collected Papers*, 2:159–78. Cf. Ostrow, *Social Sensitivity*, pp. 37–40.

18. Scheler, *The Nature of Sympathy*, pp. 140–44.

6

THEM

Besides you and me, the ordinary life-world is populated by generalized others, organized aggregates of people: antagonists, communities, and associative bodies—them, us, and it. In this and the next two chapters, I conduct phenomenologies of each—by addressing three questions: (1) What are the elementary features, the "ideal essences," of them, us, and it, respectively? (2) How do I experience myself in the presence of each? (3) How is each type generated conversationally?

THE ENEMY EXPERIENCED

"Enemy" has a host of semantic associations, finding itself variously clothed as blasphemer, rapist, beast, aggressor, stranger, or barbarian. Above all, everywhere and always the enemy stands for death.[1] Typically, enemies are visualized and mythologized either as death's instrument (that is, as a plague or an infection), as inhabiting death's archetypal residence (dirt, filth, or garbage), as death's carrier (in the form of vermin, pests, or bacilli), or as all three. More than anything else this explain how enemies come to be routinely attributed with insatiable sexual appetites, cannibalistic cravings, criminal inclinations of diabolic proportion, unimaginable powers, divine omniscience.

At least in Europe and probably elsewhere, these characteristics have been dredged from storehouses of ancient legend concerning field, mountain, and forest spirits such as Kelpies, Harpies, dwarfs, incubuses, and succubai. The leering face of Satyr is bearded, low browed, wart covered; his pointed goatlike ears, sprouting horns, and protruding genitals emphasize his voracious sexuality. The Night Huntsman has a head affixed backward on his body or has no head at all. He rides a stag-head horse, often accompanied by a female companion, Howler or Panter, so hideous that upon seeing her mortals are struck blind. Her features include a long iron nose, emblematic of her craving for the penis. As Geza Roheim says, "such spirits did not die with the ancient cultures that nurtured them. [They] live on as they did in olden times; only their names have changed."[2] Today, they are "sodomite homosexuals waiting in their lusts to rape," "Negro beasts who eat the flesh of men," "seed of Satan Jews sacrificing people in darkness."[3]

Enemies are imagined as having emerged from the "dregs" of society, from the "bowels" of the underworld. (The English "dregs" and the German *Dreck* [dung] are historically related.) They constitute an "underground" that meets surreptitiously at night in cemeteries, forests, or run-down buildings. Emerging from their holes, caverns, and grottos, they "conspire" (literally, breathe together) to dominate the world. Their plot to establish One World Government is a plan for Death itself to reign over the affairs of men

> We [shall] appear . . . as . . . saviours of the worker . . . when we propose to him to enter the ranks of . . . Socialists, Anarchists, Communists. . . . [But] we are interested in just the opposite—in [his] diminution. . . . Our power is the chronic shortness of food . . . because by . . . this . . . he is made the slave of our will, and he will not find . . . either strength or energy to set against our will.[4]

This is how the attraction of socialism to the poor is explained (and analogously, the Civil Rights movement, suffrage for women, public health programs, labor unions, and multiculturalism): all are supposed products of an insidious Plan by a secret cabal to rule the earth. Some Call it ZOG, Zionist Occupation Government. Its puppets are the "Jews-media," headquartered in Hymie Town (New York); some have trained at "Jew York University" (NYU), and work from studios in "Kosher Valley" (Hollywood), producing "politically correct" movies about "mythic" events such as the Holocaust or Anglo-Saxon crimes against Native Americans. Some labor for the ACLU to outlaw Christ from public schools; some for the American Medical Association to inoculate children with animal sera, fluoridate their drinking water, and radiate their food, thereby weakening their resistance to infection; others run banks, extending easy credit to "good, simple folk" (read: people like us) so as to mire them in debt.[5]

The enemy universally presents itself to consciousness as base, dark, smelly, foul. Those suspected of having mixed with the enemy must be avoided at all costs, for they themselves may be contaminated. To *be* the enemy is to be considered worthy of the most extreme measures: liquidation, expulsion, incineration, sterilization. Enemy zones must be "wiped out," their inhabitants "flushed" like toilets. They must be "made clean," as in the "ethnic-cleansing" program recently undertaken by Serbs against Muslims and Croats in one-time Yugoslavia; as in the Hutu slaughter of the Tutsi minority in Rawanda; as in the project of *Judenreinmachen* introduced by the Nazis in World War II ("making clean of the Jews"); or finally, as in the "wasting of 'gooks' " by the American armed forces in Vietnam. "Gook" is defined in Webster's dictionary as "a dirty, sludgy, or slimy substance." Its second meaning is "Oriental." The word "waste" has obvious excremental overtones.

The enemy is "left," what remains. What remains is garbage, rubbish, trash. Trash is refuse. To be refuse is to be deemed unacceptable. The most unacceptable condition is death. Much of what passes for domestic politics, even more what is honored in war, is only symbolic gestures to deny a place for death in the life-world, to "escape from evil."[6] This is the significance of political campaigns against sodomy, dirty books, satanic cults, witchcraft, and "drugs." In fighting against them, one saves the life-world from death.

During World War II the governor of Idaho said of the Japanese that they "live like rats, breed like rats, and act like rats." The rat is a common Western totem for death, putrefaction, and disease.

It was a term frequently applied not only to the Japanese by Americans, but also to the Jews by Germans. Other animals in the bestiary of enemies and their referents include pigs (for Jews), raccoons ('coons, for blacks), cats (for witches), dogs (for homosexuals), and goats (for satanists). Like rats, all these animals are known, at least in legend, to frequent garbage pits and to consume waste material. The *Schweinhund* or "swine-dog," a particularly repellent creature, was still another Jewish icon for the Nazi.

MYSELF IN THE ENEMY'S PRESENCE

The enemy presents itself to me as diabolic—"diabolic" meaning "that thrown apart" (*dia* = apart + *bolos* = thrown). In other words, it is something alien to me, other than me. If the enemy is "left," as indicated above, then I am "right." I am right-eous. If the enemy is filth, then I am clean; and if the enemy is death, I am life. Here, in brief, is glimpsed the perennial fascination of enemies.

In marking out, isolating, and destroying the anathema (*ana* = counter + *thema* = themes) in our midst, the mores, values, and customs we share are corrected, purified, rejuvenated. As Georg Simmel pointed out long ago, this is precisely the "social function" of enemies. They serve as scapegoats. In being "thrown apart" from us by exile, imprisonment, and murder, the group is redeemed from mortality.[7] This is why Simmel can say that as old enemies recede on the horizon—in our times the "Evil Empire," the USSR—it is always the better part of wisdom to devise new ones to take their place: Grenadan revolutionaries, Panamanian strongman Manuel Noriega, Moammar Khaddafi, Saddam Hussein.[8] The presence of enemies cleanses befouled air, and breathes new life into previously indolent, self-absorbed peoples.

In ancient Greece there were two words for the scapegoat, *pharmakon* and *katharma*. Both have English derivatives, "pharmacy" and "cathartic," which display uncanny understandings of the nature of enemies. *Pharmakon* was the name given the sacrificial victim killed during the Festival of Thargelia in May. The victim was drawn from a stable of old, poor, deviant individuals, many of them women, kept at public expense for this very purpose.[9] Like a medicinal substance, the *pharmakon* was spoken of as a poison the destruction of which serves as an "antidote" for the ills of the polis: the bitter disputes, pettiness, rumors, and anxieties that have accumulated like a sickness during the Winter months. In killing the poison the community is "cured" of its ills. (Compare this to the Christian Jesus who is said to have taken on the sins of the world and died, also in spring, so that humanity as a whole might be saved.)

Katharma is even more revealing in this respect. It refers to a foul substance the extraction of which from the individual's body purges it, cleanses it, and gives it health. The result of this action is *katharsis*. *Katharsis* means not just the display of emotions, but more directly the movement of the bowels by purging. Hence, the English "cathartic," that which relieves dyspepsia and constipation. Understood this way, the Greek *katharma* is compacted waste material produced by the body politic, the evacuation of which alleviates stress and provides relief for the citizenry.

THE MAKING OF ENEMIES

Enemies are ordinarily experienced in the natural attitude as having existences independent of our consciousness of them. Our hatred is viewed as a natural reaction to what they already were prior to our happening on the scene, namely, dealers-in-death. This is clearly evident in one of the German words for "enemy," *Erbfiende*, literally "enemy from birth." This is revulsion toward a particular people (Slavs, Frenchmen, or Jews) so deep-seated and visceral that it seems born into the average patriot. In reality, however, we are accomplices in the making of our antagonists; like all beings they emerge from conversation about them. This assertion needs qualification, however.

The label "enemy" can affix itself to anyone who chances in the way of shrieking gossip about "who is to blame" for a plague, a local rape, a drought, and so forth.[10] As proof of this, John Dollard and his cohorts once demonstrated that the frequency of Negro lynchings in the Deep South was inversely correlated with the price of cotton.[11] If innocent, vulnerable populations are always at risk of being cast as evil-doers in dramas of social regeneration, it is also true that the vile deeds and words of some render them available to receive enemy projections: Hitler, Stalin, Genghis Khan, and Timur the Lame come to mind. To be sure, it is perilously difficult to determine who "deserves" classification as a bona fide agent of death. This is no excuse for failing to discriminate altogether. It is a mistake to imagine that by "swallowing" our own evil projections (by refusing to diabolize altogether), we will be preserved miraculously from violation.[12] After all, just because people are paranoid does not mean that others are not out to get them. Evil is a mystery ultimately insusceptible to therapeutic interventions. It is already there, part of the "gift of Being" written of earlier—to be "lived," but never fully resolved.

However this may be, there is a definite shop of implements drawn upon in the fabrication of enemies. These include the public naming of a people as fiends of one sort or another through gossip and editorializing; the devising of myths to demonstrate why they "must" be what they are, namely, instances of death and putrefaction; and finally, there is the passing-on of these narratives in classroom, church, and media so that they are received as part of the common stock of knowledge about the world.[13] Perhaps the most important of these enemy-making tools is the piacular rite.

Like most forms of human communication, rituals "talk" not only by words, but by spectacle, tactile sensation, scent, and music. The main difference between ritual talk and other conversation forms is that ordinary discourse is spontaneous, or at least it appears so. Ritual, on the other hand, is prefixed. It employs practiced gesture and utterance, the manipulation of paraphernalia by persons specially delegated ahead of time for the purpose, wearing predesignated vestments, and conducting the affair at preset, "sacred," times and places. This is true whether it be a religious sacrament, a nominating convention, a commencement exercise, or a piacular rite.

"Piacularity" is the archaic English term for criminality. As used here "piacular rite" refers to a ceremony that atones for wrongdoing and expiates evil.[14] It comes from the Latin *piaculum*, which means sin offering, the victim sacrificed for the community's wellbeing. In America such rites include criminal and juvenile court proceedings, courts-martial, insanity hearings, church excommunications, grand juries, impeachments, or other tribunals whose task it is to indict.

To use Harold Garfinkel's phrase, all piacular rites ultimately involve "ceremonial degradation."[15] Their purpose is to elevate the community and its standards of morality, beauty, and reason by formally debasing a problematic individual or group—this by determining it to be heretical, criminal, delinquent, or mad.

According to Garfinkel, several conditions are required for the successful performance of any piacular rite. First, the accusers (physicians, priests, prosecutors, counselors) must testify by word and document that nothing in the piaculum's life is accidental, but rather is an index of his or her perversity. Even citations of the person's law-abiding normality must be reinterpreted to confirm his or her essential abnormality. "True, he appeared to act sanely at the time, but in fact this is another symptom of his sickness." "True, he claims to have converted to Christianity, but this is merely a ruse to manipulate the jury." Second, this abnormality must be rhetorically counterpoised to its opposite—of which the accusers themselves must be examples: sanity, professionalism, objectivity, piety. Third, the accusers must demonstrate that they are not moved by private considerations of profit, revenge, or fear, but act solely out of concern for "tribal values."

Neither society, nor even most corporate bodies, can flourish long without piacular ceremonies. Rene Girard has gone so far as to argue that they are the most important engines of social order.[16] The integrity of the life-world cannot be sustained, he says, without the periodic "throwing apart" of a designated piaculum from amidst the tribe.

CONCLUSION

Recently, American ceremonial throwings-apart have taken one of two forms depending on how the protagonists imagine the Nation.

The first group conceives of the United States as an exclusive, "Christian" country. Its diabolic other therefore assumes attributes of the anti-Christ, however else it may differ. The permutations are virtually endless: from ATMs to MTV, from commercial bar codes to postal zip codes, from Darwinism to deism, from labor unions to the Union of Concerned Scientists, from Walkman stereos to Teenage Mutant Ninja Turtles, from popery and Pete Seeger to pop, from the National Council of Churches to Freemasonry, from the United Nations to the National Council of Churches, and beyond.[17] Besides sharing the appellation "anti-Christ" these items are alike in being symptomatic of the "juggernaut of modernity," as Anthony Giddens has called it, of forces that seem to undermine the integrity of local neighborhoods, imperil faith, and shatter families. In talking about, being terrified by, and mounting campaigns against the symptoms of this beastly power, America's "fundamentals" are validated. Certainty is found in an uncertain world.

For those whose image of America is more universal and inclusive, on the other hand, the enemy is pictured as an opponent of globalization, free trade, and diversity; one whose brow furrows with concern when talk turns to the need for tolerating racial, linguistic, or sexual "differences." This enemy is rarely accused of being an anti-Christ. Instead, the indictment against the enemy revolves around their alleged backwardness, provincialism, close-mindedness, or plain old stupidity. At best, they are pictured as paranoid, and are supposedly treatable by a palliative regime of counseling, sensitivity-training, and doses of anti-anxiety pills. At worst, they are fantasized as camouflaged militants, who scurry about in darkness answering to names like xenophobe, tribalist, nationalist, racialist, Nazi: folks best dealt with by undercover agents and threats of imprisonment. Whether they are sick or criminal, there is pride in knowing that compared to them, we are certifiably progressive and forward looking, confident and well adjusted, prepared to step buoyantly into the twenty-first century.

NOTES

1. James Aho, *This Thing of Darkness: A Sociology of the Enemy* (Seattle: University of Washington Press, 1994), pp. 107–21. For amplification, see Norman Brown, *Life against Death* (Middletown, CT: Wesleyan University Press, 1973).

2. Geza Roheim, *The Riddle of the Sphinx* (New York: Harper and Row, 1974 [1934]), p. 35. See also, pp. 1–43.

3. These titles are taken from *Prepare War* (Pontiac, MO: Covenant, Sword and the Arm of the Lord Bookstore, n.d.). For "proof" that Jews indeed fit this defamatory title, see Arnold Leese, *Jewish Ritual Murder* (London: International Fascist League, 1938). For a general study of these and related figures, see Sam Keen, *Faces of the Enemy: Reflections of the Hostile Imagination* (San Francisco: Harper and Row, 1986).

4. *The Protocols of the Learned Elders of Zion*, trans. Victor Marsden (n.p. 1905), protocol 3. For the sources and validity of this document, see Aho, *This Thing of Darkness*, pp. 78–82.

5. For these and related conspiracies, see James Aho, *The Politics of Righteousness* (Seattle: University of Washington Press, 1990), pp. 91–92, 264–66.

6. The foremost study of these efforts is Ernest Becker's, *Escape from Evil* (New York: Free Press, 1975).

7. Georg Simmel, *Conflict and the Web of Group Affiliations*, trans. Kurt Wolff and Reinhard Bendix (Glencoe, IL: Free Press, 1955), p. 98.

8. Aho, *This Thing of Darkness*, pp. 83–104.

9. James G. Frazer, *The Golden Bough* (New York: Macmillan, 1951 [1922]), pp. 633–60.

10. For a tragic example, see Aho, *This Thing of Darkness*, pp. 35–49.

11. John Dollard et al., *Frustration and Aggression* (New Haven, CT: Yale University Press, 1939).

12. Aho, *This Things of Darkness*, pp. 17–20, 120–21.

13. Ibid., pp. 27–32.

14. For piacular rites in general, see Emile Durkheim, *The Elementary Forms of Religious Life*, trans. Joseph Ward Swain (Glencoe, IL: Free Press, 1969).

15. Harold Garfinkel, "Conditions of Successful Degradation Ceremonies," *American Journal of Sociology* 61 (1956): 420–24.

16. Rene Girard, *Violence and the Sacred*, trans. Patrick Gregory (Baltimore, MD: Johns Hopkins University Press, 1977), pp. 93–96.

17. Robert Fuller, *Naming the Antichrist* (New York: Oxford University Press, 1995), pp. 227–28.

7

Us

THE COMMUNITY EXPERIENCE

Enemies are those who by negation inform me that I am morally upright. Communities are the others with whom I identify and for whom the pronouns "we" and "us" are fitting.

Anything held in common can serve as a basis for we-ness: shared speech, a job, religious devotion, sexual preference, a shared recreation, the amount of melanin in our skins, a natural disaster, a debilitating disease, or death. Consider these words of the nineteenth-century German philosopher Heinrich von Treitschke: "Nothing unites a nation more closely than war. . . . [For] war, with all its brutality and sternness, weaves a bond of love between man and man, linking them together to face death."[1]

Fifty years later, reflecting on his own experience in the trenches of World War I, Martin Heidegger would confirm this sentiment: "The nearness of death . . . stood before each one . . . so that this could become the source of unconditioned belonging-together. Precisely death, which each . . . must die for himself, . . . creates the space of community from which comradeship arises."[2]

Sociologists often equate "community" with the German word *Gemeinschaft. Gemeinschaft* denotes a sense of solidarity growing either from shared "blood," from attachment to a common land, or from a people's devotion to the same cause. Ferdinand Toennies writes of these, respectively, as the "vegetative heart," the "animal soul," and the "human soul" of *Gemeinschaft*.[3] Whatever its source, those who believe themselves a community tend to act out of a sense of duty, love, or affection toward it, with little thought of what it might cost (or benefit) them as individuals.[4] This is because a community is experienced as my own symbolic extension. Its fate bears directly on how I feel about myself. When we prosper, I too feel expansive. When we are threatened or when we lose, I am diminished.

It is important to emphasize that as used here "community" does not refer to a specific grouping as such: to rural towns, neighborhoods, gangs, or teams. Rather, it refers to how groupings are, to use Toennies's term, intended or "willed" by their members—how they disclose themselves to consciousness. Failure to recognize this has led many commentators mistakenly to suppose that the spread of bureaucracies, factories, and metropolises in modern society has "eclipsed" the possibility of community.[5] Research on "urban villagers" and the persistence of nationalism and racism, to say nothing of cult formation and fundamentalist sectarianism, unqualifiably demonstrate the error in this line of thinking.[6] Amidst even the most impersonal and hierarchically arranged corporations, armies, prisons, and schools, community not only survives, it flourishes.

Romantic traditionalists extoll the family as an example of community belonging. Its possessions are said to be effortlessly shared; there is a high degree of trust among its members; each "feels the others' pains." In short, it is spoken of as more than a means for aggrandizing egotistic interests. It is something "affirmed in its essence," to paraphrase Toennies, an end in itself. Field observation, however, frequently confutes this portrait. Members of the same biological unit may feel in fact that they have virtually nothing in common; that they have been irredeemably betrayed by the very persons who earlier had sworn to them their eternal fidelity, and whose emotional displays, as a result, turn hearts to stone. Funerals and reunions, when not altogether avoidable, are experienced as compulsory affairs, painfully contrived, emotionally draining. Here, family is no longer a "we," but something closer to an "it," a temporary association of convenience.[7] To reiterate, whether or not a social unit is communal, does not depend on its size, locale, or purpose, but on how its members are conscious of it.

Many Americans view the nation-state as little more than a body of "pointy-headed" bureaucrats headquartered in Washington, D.C., whose only contact with them is through stultifying regulations and the IRS. On the other hand, nineteenth-century German political theorists celebrated their own government as the preeminent form of community: "the community (*Gemeinschaft*) of men asserting itself in action," to quote one of them. The German Nazi party resuscitated this idea with a popular jingle, *Gemeindenutz vor Eigennutz!* (Community good before private good!). In Nazi doctrine, people were said to be truly free only when their wills coincided with that of the *Gemeinstaat* (the community-state). Now they would yearn to do that commanded of them by the party.

ME IN THE PRESENCE OF WE

Whether I see myself as part of a neighborhood gang called the Skull Brothers, or as a member of Greenpeace, or share with my companions only a craving for alcohol, when in community I feel grounded, anchored, secure in the life-world. Knut Hamsun describes the Norwegian peasantry in these terms: "Look at you folk at Sellanrää . . . rooted deep in the past. There you are, . . . in touch with heaven and earth, one with them, one with all these wide, deep-rooted things."[8]

In community I know my place in time and space, and this is with "my folk." In their company at the club house, political convention, or bar, my existence once again becomes meaningful, directed, significant. "I was lucky to have known them," says poet-essayist John Haines of his Alaskan compatriots. "They were my people, . . . and the best of them I have loved with a deep appreciation that has never left me. . . . When I think of them now, it is of something hugely tender and forgiving, akin to a healing thingness in the world that assures the soil of its grasses, the earth of its sun."[9]

The rootedness emblematic of community originates from a conviction that what we have in common is fundamental to our being. For Hamsun and Haines this is the land on which a folk has dwelt for countless years. Here, the brooks, cliffs, and caverns in which their children play are the same ones their parents knew in their youth, and here, too, the blood of their families is so mixed that everyone shares facial features, hair color, and body type. This is the soil from which each has sprung, the glens, hillocks and creeks to which they affix their names—Raymond, Mason, Dayton, Elma—and to which they look forward to returning at their deaths. The German peasant word *Gemeinde* resonates with these primeval meanings, as does, "mother-" and "fatherland."

In community a feeling of intimate familiarity with my comrades prevails. After all, we are "family." Hence, the understandable compulsion to address them metaphorically in kinship terms: "sister," "sis," "brother," "bro'," "papa," "mama." Just as I was born into a biological family, it seems reasonable to speak of being "reborn" into or "wedded" to my community.

Figurative rebirths and marriages typically are memorialized by rites of passage. While variable in content, they share standard features.[10] Initiates first take leave of the "womb" of ordinary existence, discarding their "children's" garments. They next move through a limbo state wherein they are neither who they once were nor yet a "new man," a brother. At this point there may be the spilling of blood, if not by the initiates themselves (as in the so-called jumping-in characteristic of American teen-girl gangs), then by a victim chosen for this purpose (as in the drive-by snipings of random street-goers by their teen-boy counterparts). Once admitted to the "family," initiates may be offered apparel and names appropriate to their born-again status.

The solidarity I feel with my companions is experienced as a diffuse, ultimately undischargeable debt. This is because I sense that my community has "made me what I am today." "Were it not for them, I wouldn't be here." Her concern and encouragement gives me strength, her affection, pride. Thus, whether we are bonded in our being AIDS victims, members of an Al-Anon support group, or members of the same faith, I feel obligated out of piety and loyalty to her, even if this entails great cost to me.

As both Thomistic moral philosophy and Confucianism understood, piety is not identical to justice.[11] In a just relationship one merely gives back (or receives) in accordance to what they have taken or given. Justice is a product of calculation and is therefore eminently rational. Community solidarity in contrast rests on something more than quid pro quo exchanges between individuals. It requires that companions give back *more* than what is mathematically owed. The gratuitous mercy shown by a judge in a criminal court may be an expression of piety—certainly, the willingness of citizen-soldiers to die for their country is. Both mercy and patriotism originate from an awareness of the impossibility of ever being able fully to repay one's accrued debts. No matter what one gives, it is never enough. If the icon for justice is a balance held by the blindfolded Themis, then that for piety is the Madonna cradling her child.

While the loving embrace of community secures me in the lifeworld, it simultaneously enfolds me, confines me, limits me in my individuality. This is the downside, if it can be so stated, of community. I can be many things in community: guided, protected, accepted, nourished. One thing I can never be is that most celebrated of modern things, a fully self-actualized ego. This point will be elaborated on in the next chapter.

MANUFACTURING COMMUNITY

Communities, like enemies, are built from discourse in the broadest sense: from pledges of loyalty to the group, and self-condemnatory oaths; from agonizing discussions about "our" problems; from reflections on the "good old days," especially remembrances of "our" founding. There is first of all the conversational identification—the labeling—of an aggregate of individuals (by themselves or others) as members of such and community: "Christian patriots," "Mormons," "gays." Next comes mythic elaboration, by which the (often imaginary) features of the group are shown to have deep historic, perhaps biological, roots. Finally, these legends are embedded in the minds of younger generations in the form of school lessons, homilies, and fireside chats. When this happens, the designated community begins to be experienced in an alienated way, as a natural fact instead of as the art-fact it is.

Crucial to the formation and maintenance of community are rituals, specifically, ritual communions. These have many of the features of piacular rites, including formal vestments, sacred times and places, incense, formulaic utterances, and music. Indeed, some communions contain a piacular element, as will be seen below. Nonetheless, there is an important difference between how communions and piacular rites accomplish their goals. Piacular rites bring people together by dramatically displaying what they are *not*, namely, "them," the diabolic, those who have been "thrown apart"; communions achieve the same end by vividly affirming what they have in common.

So, in a pageant reminiscent of the Eleusian mysteries of Demeter and Persephone, symbols of the annual death and resurrection of plant life, the little logging town of Shelton, Washington, pays homage to the surrounding woods, its communal base, with a spring ritual called the Forest Festival. In it, the prettiest senior high schoolers are chosen to serve as the forest queen and her court. Like the virgin Persephone, they are kidnapped and ensconced in a burned-out snag by middle school boys suitably arrayed in red. The stage lights dim. This is death. Now comes the battle between the fire devils and their white-shirted, pulaski-hefting antagonists. As evil is beaten into submission, Paul Bunyan, a strapping teen, is led to the place of imprisonment by a benign elf. Grade schoolers, as squirrels, deer, birds, and forest nymphs, emerge from the shadows to celebrate the victory. Older classmates, costumed to represent the town's ethnicities—Poles, Germans, and Swedes—joyfully dance polkas, schottisches, and waltzes.

Each citizen in his or her own way participates in the festival: the high school band accompanies the performance, ending with "Pomp and Circumstance," as Paul Bunyan crowns the queen and leads her offstage to an imagined marriage; teachers choreograph the whole affair and spend weeks training their charges in their respective roles; mothers, as ever, are behind the scenes at their sewing machines; fathers manage the stage. The men's celebration is the next day, when in contests of tree topping, birling, truck driving, and log bucking, they display their virility and skill. In this way the community of Shelton is renewed for one more year.[12]

Race

A perennially salient basis for community formation in America has been race. While ordinarily races are experienced in the natural attitude as biologically given, in actuality they are social constructs. Thus, we can write of the "invention" of the Negro (jointly by apologists for slavery and by proponents of Afrocentrism); the "construction" of the Jew (by Zionists and anti-Semites alike); or the "creation" of the American Indian by Hollywood filmmakers and Anglo "wannabes."[13]

To be sure, there is almost always a grain of truth in stereotypes, including racial stereotypes. However, except for a few diseases like sickle-cell anemia and food intolerances (such as that of Orientals to milk), scientists are hard pressed to associate differences in complexion, height, eye form, nose width, or hair texture (all of which are used as racial counters) with anything other than individual idiosyncracies. Even less can visible racial indexes by themselves explain variations between people in terms of foot speed and endurance, math wizardry, law-abidingness and civility, sexual prowess, muscular coordination, emotional sensitivity, or rhythm. However, this is precisely what racists, which is to say, believers in the natural ontology of race, claim to be able to do.

The following comments are intended to destabilize the natural attitude toward race by phenomenologically "destroying" it in the sense discussed in the first chapter. This is done by dismantling that much ballyhooed and maligned figure, "white man"—showing the probable origin of the signifier itself, and then tracing the arbitrary use of the term, and its ritual dramatization.

According to historian Theodore Allen, the first Africans to arrive in the New World in 1620 were not greeted by people identifying themselves as "white," but as Englishmen. Indeed, the first documented mention of "white man," at least in American law, would not appear until some two generations later in the Virginia Statutes of 1691–1705, in an article entitled "Concerning Slaves and Servants."[14] Here, the Irish are characterized as "white" (albeit savage and heathenish, read: Catholic), and are granted civil rights as temporary, indentured, servants. Africans, as "black," are relegated to the status of permanent bond chattel and accorded no human rights (although owners are urged to treat them as prudently as they would any investment). Allen's argument is that this distinction was calculatedly made to discourage Irish bondsmen from allying with their African peers against their common master. Bacon's Rebellion of 1676 had presumably alerted English plantation owners of the danger such an alliance might constitute to their own rule.

Whether Allen's explanation of the decisive statute is accurate or not, his general account of events underscores the point to made here, namely, that the fundamental racial divisions taken for granted in America today as natural are traceable to a conversational moment. The term "white man" was originally devised as a rhetorical weapon by persons with a vested interest in turning Americans against each other.

It is not necessary here to detail the myths concocted after the fact to legitimize the enslavement of "blacks," for example, that they have no souls and hence are not truly human. What is important to note is that an equally elaborate mythology emerged around the category "white" to legitimize the privileges routinely accorded its claimants. Among these were stories concerning the alleged origins of white man, racial genealogies. Table 7.1 outlines two of these genealogies.

The information in the left column was promulgated in the nineteenth century by British Israelites, as they were then known (more on this below). That in the right column has been disseminated for over half a century by the Church of Jesus Christ Christian-Aryan Nations, one of this country's most notorious "Christian Identity" (CI) congregations.[15]

CI is so called because it alleges that the true ancestors of "white" people were the ancient Israelites. This presumably explains why they are "God's chosen people," and hence why it is that they have come to rule earth. In short, "whites" are merely carrying out the biblical order issued to them by God to be "Judah's Scepter." In CI Jews are adjudged "Satan's Kids," imposters, sons of Cain, history's first murderer. As for "black," "brown," "yellow," and "red" men, they are reviled as "muds," peoples whose pigmentations betray their earthly origins (as well as their excremental essence).

CI is viciously exclusionary. Yet, when compared to the British Israelite theology from which it arose, it represents a surprising

Table 7.1
Two Racial Genealogies

Nation	Genealogical Origins According to	
	British Israelism	Christian Identity*
Britain	All ten lost tribes of Israel	Ephraim only
Ireland	Celts	Ephraim
Germany	Teutons	Judah
Holland	Celts	Reuben
Denmark	Teutons, Huns	Dan
Norway	Teutons, Huns	Napthali
Iceland	Teutons, Huns	Benjamin
Sweden	Teutons, Huns	Asher
Finland	Mongols	Issachar
Russia	Tartars	Zebulum
Spain	Moors, Saracens	Simeon
Italy	Berbers, Goths	Gad

*The tribe of Levi is said to be "scattered among all nations." The United States is considered either Manasseh (Ephraim's "twin brother") or the final gathering place of all the tribes, thus the land promised Israel, to be cleansed of all "colored" peoples.

degree of racial ecumenism. British Israelism, for example, insists that the British alone are Israelites. Only they are "white and delightsome" to the Lord. This is proven to its satisfaction by the fact that "British" is (allegedly) a conjunction of two Hebrew words, *b'rith* (covenant) and *ish* (people). Furthermore, British Israelism holds that the Irish, the Germans, the Scandinavians, and the Dutch are all descendants of alien, nonwhite races. The high cheek bones, epicanthic eye folds, olive skins, and black hair, respectively, of Finns, Slavs, Spaniards, and Italians are explained by their having intermixed with Mongols, Saracens, Berbers, or Moors.

Christian Identity sees the racial world in a different light. First, it reduces Britain to the status of just *one* of the thirteen Israelite tribes. Second, it insists that the English and the Irish have the same legendary ancestor, Ephraim. Hence, they constitute the same race. Third and most importantly, peoples who in British Israelism are excluded entirely from consideration as "white" are now embraced as blood brothers. The one-time "yellow" Finns have become "white" folk descended from the tribe of Issachar; the "brown" Spanish are now a "white" folk whose lineage is traceable to the tribe of Simeon; and so on with the Italians, the Russians, and the Poles: they too are now "white men."[16]

Were racial categories truly grounded in biology, persons of the same gene pool could not move from one race to the next. Racial boundaries would remain fixed. However, far from being impermeable and definite, they are fluid and malleable.[17] This, more than any other consideration, demonstrates the contrived nature of race.

Although the means by which people come to understand they are members of a race vary, probably the most powerful is the communal rite. This is because ritual affects more than the higher cognitive functions. It impacts the limbic psyche as well. Rituals are not just heard; they are seen, smelled, and touched—hence, the significance of Kwanzaa, a week-long festival of gift giving and shared meals, conceived of in 1966 in New York to sensitize dark-skinned Americans to their African roots (from Swahili for first fruits). There are also ceremonials developed to remind light-skinned Americans of their "race." The following was witnessed in the late 1980s in Idaho at Aryan Nations headquarters.[18]

> On a warm, sultry summer night, out of the recesses of a thick fir forest, a single file of white-robed men, women, and children eerily emerge, led by two torch bearers. Two hundred in number, all deathly still. Some wear high conical hats masking their faces and cut with round black eye holes; most are bareheaded. Among them I notice several with whom earlier that afternoon I had easily bantered. Now their visages are grim and focused.
>
> A blue-shirted usher directs the single line of sheeted spec-

ters, half to his left, half to his right. Moving now in opposite directions, each led by a torch bearer, the lines form two circles, one encompassing the other, the inner circle having a diameter of about 100 feet. They are arrayed around a 30-foot-tall kerosene-soaked, rag-enshrouded wooden cross.

Near the base of the cross a small bonfire has been lit. Four celebrants step forward making a straight line in front of the bonfire. One wears black vestments embroidered with white, and a cardinal's miter. He will serve as high priest. Another is in a brown, open-jacketed seersucker leisure suit and white shirt; a third resembles a German *Luftwaffe* colonel, complete with jodhpurs, knee-high riding boots, officer's cap, pistol belt, and medals; the last personifies a Protestant minister with business suit and red tie. Blue-shirted guards are positioned at occasional points inside the circles, some cradling rifles, others holding flags of the various Aryan nations.

The first priest dips a fagot into the fire, ignites it, turns and ceremonially hands it to the concelebrant on his right; he in turn passes it to the third, and he to the high priest. The last, then, with flaming torch steps to the base of the cross and touches it. An explosion of fire. Night turns into midday.

Although I am standing some distance from the spectacle at the wood's edge, my face warms with the heat. I search to give my feelings words. The first that comes to mind is "power"! In terror mixed with shame at my naiveté, I realize I have for too long dismissed these people as frequenters of a harmless diversionary lark. This rite I witness goes back centuries; it connects the participants not only with each other in the present but with their ancestors in the past. For a moment I understand for the first time how race is truly rejuvenated; not by books and posters, but by drama.

The high priest, in a voice resembling that of a bishop explaining to the assembled throng the meaning of a sacrament, to calm their fears at seeing something so odd, describes the meaning of the burning cross. This is not, he intones, a symbol of racial violence; nor is it desecration of a Christian icon. It is instead a sign of mutuality and defense. Its source is the Celtic practice of lighting seacoast pyres as guide signals. It has, he says, become "a light to guide the white in the darkness of these times."

The assembly is asked to recall vows undertaken to aid wives whose husbands languish in prison and children without fathers. Those who transgress these obligations, he warns, are to be punished by death as betrayers of the race.

NOTES

1. Heinrich von Treitschke, *Politics*, trans. Blanche Dugdale and Torben de Bille (New York: Harcourt, Brace and World, 1963), pp. 59, 245.

2. Martin Heidegger, *Gesamtausgabe*, vol. 39, in Michael Zimmerman, *Heidegger's Confrontation with Modernity* (Bloomington: Indiana University Press, 1990), p. 73.

3. Ferdinand Toennies, *Community and Society*, trans. Charles Loomis (East Lansing: Michigan State University Press, 1957).

4. Besides Toennies, the following account is also indebted to Herbert Spiegelberg, "On the Right to Say 'We': A Linguistic and Phenomenological Analysis," in *Phenomenological Sociology*, ed. George Psathas (New York: John Wiley & Sons, 1973), pp. 129–58.

5. See Maurice Stein, *The Eclipse of Community* (New York: Harper and Row, 1964), for a survey of this pessimistic literature.

6. For example, see Michael Novak, *The Rise of the Unmeltable Ethnics* (New York: Macmillan, 1975); Herbert Gans, *Urban Villagers* (New York: Free Press, 1962); and particularly, Joseph Gusfield, *Community: A Critical Response* (New York: Harper and Row, 1975).

7. See Margaret Talbot's "Dial-a-Wife," *New Yorker*, 20 & 27 October 1997, pp. 196–208.

8. Knut Hamsun, *Growth of the Soil*, trans. W. W. Worster (New York: Vintage Books, 1972 [1921]).

9. John Haines, *The Stars, the Snow, the Fire* (St. Paul, MN: Greywolf, 1989), p. 164.

10. Mircea Eliade, *Rites and Symbols of Initiation* (New York: Harper and Row, 1958).

11. Josef Pieper, *The Four Cardinal Virtues* (Notre Dame, IN: Notre Dame University Press, 1966), pp. 104–13.

12. During my childhood and youth, I participated in the Forest Festival variously as chipmunk, fire fighter, folk dancer, and orchestra member. For the background of the Festival, see Murray Morgan, *The Last Wilderness* (Seattle: University of Washington Press, 1955), pp. 189–214.

13. For example, see Hunt King, "Inventing the Indian: White Images,

Oral Literature, and Contemporary Native Writers" (Ph.D. diss., University of Utah, 1986); Kathleen Neils-Conzen, "German Americans and the Invention of Ethnicity," in *Germans in America*, ed. Randall Miller (Philadelphia, PA: German Society of America, 1984); Eric Hobsbawm and Terence Ranger, eds., *The Invention of Tradition*, (Cambridge, UK: Cambridge University Press, 1983).

14. Theodore Allen, *The Invention of the White Race* (New York: Verso, 1994).

15. Michael Barkun, *Religion and the Racist Right: The Origins of the Christian Identity Movement* (Chapel Hill: University of North Carolina Press, 1994).

16. James Aho, *The Politics of Righteousness* (Seattle: University of Washington Press, 1990), pp. 83–113.

17. Allen, *The Invention of the White Race*, p. 27. In Hispanic colonies it was possible to become white merely by purchasing a royal certificate of "whiteness," regardless of one's complexion.

Nor are racial categories irrevocable. Native Americans were once widely viewed as racially connected to Europeans. In time they transmogrified into "red men," see Alden Vaughan, "From White Man to Redskin: Changing Anglo-American Perceptions of the American Indian," *American Historical Journal* 87 (October 1982): 917–53.

18. James Aho, "The Recent Ethnogenesis of 'White Man,' " *Left Bank* 5 (1993): 55–64.

8

IT

THE ESSENCE OF ASSOCIATION

An association is a relationship entered into not for itself, but for purposes apart, notably power or profit. As for community, what determines whether or not a grouping is associative is how it reveals itself to its participants. The Japanese factory is based partly on a feudal management model known as *ningen kankej* (social relationships). In this each worker is expected to give his or her undying loyalty and subservience to the company in exchange for lifetime tenure and the provision of all the accoutrements of welfare and comfort.[1] Thus, while it may appear from a distance to be entirely associatively based, to the employees themselves it has a communal ambience.

IBM in America has experimented with the same principle: offering permanent job security to its workers, underwriting retraining expenses, and providing them low interest company-subsidized loans, among other things. In return the workers are expected to devote their entire careers to the so-called family. Even *looking* elsewhere for employment is considered a betrayal of one's obligations.

This is not unique to IBM. The Human Relations movement, inaugurated by Elton Mayo during the 1930s, seeks to foster an atmosphere of medieval togetherness on the factory floor—this, by promoting laid-back, open-door managerial styles; decision making by consensus; dispute-mediation procedures; sensitivity training; and Dilbert-style euphemisms to describe the nastier side of work (like firing people): "offering early retirement," "rightsizing," "creating career change opportunities," "upgrading," and so forth. "Re-creat[ing] the belongingness of the Middle Ages" is said to enhance worker morale, lower absentee rates, and ensure high levels of productivity.[2]

Credit must go to Max Weber for first elucidating the phenomenological features of associations, which he considered "the most rational means of control over human beings" ever devised.[3] His protégé, Talcott Parsons, would later systematize these into the "action orientation" of bureaucracies, the ways in which they are typically thought and seen: universalism, specificity, achievement, and neutrality.[4] (1) The obligations of associates extend no further than their "job descriptions." These are detailed in statute books and provide *universal* (as opposed to particularistic) standards by which performance is measured. Associates are subject to termination only for incompetency or dereliction of duty. (2) Said duties are continually "upgraded," that is, functionally delimited and *specified* so as to "maximize utilization of 'human resources.' " (3) Associates receive appointments solely on the basis of their individual *achievements* as evidenced by scores on competitive exams, satisfactory supervisory reports, and seniority. (4) Associates approach their work with affective *neutrality*, that is, in an attitude of emotional detachment. To promote impersonalism, associates neither own their tools nor their offices, and are paid a fixed salary instead of receiving gifts, benefices, or favors.

Modern armies, businesses, churches, hospitals, charities, and political parties may have different purposes, but all are cast from the same associative mold, which Weber likens to an "iron cage." As such they have comparable psychological impacts on those subject to their authority. These impacts are enumerated in a literary genre known as existential phenomenology, a style of reflection concerned with how I am for the most part while in "it," the company or the firm.

MYSELF IN ASSOCIATION

Existentialism is not merely a consequence of bureaucratization.[5] Several of its themes were evident as far back as the Book of Job. Any institution that encourages egotism is fertile soil for existential sensibilities. Among those mentioned in chapter 4 are men's barracks, hero myths, sacramental penance, and individual civil rights. Nevertheless, as an identifiable movement, existentialism appeared under that name only after World War II, and then among avant garde European intellectuals. It arose partly from their experiences as soldiers, clerks, party functionaries, hospital aides, and middle-level corporate officials.

Egoism, Loneliness, and Other-Directedness

The human product of associative life is ego, a person for whom all ethical questions reduce to "what's in it for me?"[6] If ego senses obligations to others, as it occasionally does, it is only so far as it has contracted with them to exchange things. "Economics" for ego is the science of self-aggrandizement; its confession, the "Church of Me"; its politics, the "Me Party."[7]

In the presence of equally solipsistic others, ego experiences itself alone. The very problem of how ego can know others' minds, dealt with in chapter 5, documents ego's isolation. Starting from what it takes as the only indubitable datum—"I am"—ego finds it difficult to imagine other people as anything but derivations of itself. To ego, "you" are at best my own project(ion). I make you out of my own mental contents.

Existential loneliness is not the same as solitude, which might encourage contemplative inwardness and cognizance of one's secret desires and true originality. It is, instead, the feeling of being "out of place," of not being part of the Everybody, the crowd. For paradoxically, although ego is narcissistic, it is equally "other-directed."[8] It is obsessed with what the public thinks, particularly with what ego imagines it thinks about him.

Of course, whether they are involved in associations or not, all human beings are solicitous of others' opinions. Other-directedness, however, refers to an expression of this natural proclivity peculiar to the functionary. In fact Heidegger's term for other-directedness is translatable as "officialness" or "publicness" (*Offentlichkeit*). Public man, he says, subjects himself to the whims of the Everybody (*das Man*) because of his own self-absorption. That is, insofar as he has so little grasp of the source of his own authenticity, he must rely on "they" to tell him how to dress, what to eat, how to relax, and what to believe. "[He] takes pleasure . . . as *they* take pleasure; see[s], read[s], and judge[s] . . . literature and art as *they* [do]; . . . shrink[s] back from the 'great mass' as *they* shrink back; . . . find[s] 'shocking' what *they* find shocking."[9]

Having little to stand for in itself, public man (or increasingly, woman) determines its value invidiously, by comparing its achievements to those of the crowd. This accounts for its involvement in two characteristic activities: gossip—by means of which it learns the latest fads, tastes, celebrities, and scandals; and self-advertisement—by which it displays to the crowd its capacity to "keep up." The dramaturgic metaphor mentioned in chapter 4 fascinates public man because it vividly reiterates to him the experience of being his own salesman. To public man everything is "image," and crucial to a successful image is "personality," a facade of affability and well-adjustedness.

Transiency, Homelessness, and Angst

The monad is a nomad. Perpetually attuned to its next big chance, ego migrates in and out of relationships, therapies, causes, careers, and locales, alighting only long enough to reprovision its bags. If spatial movement proves momentarily impossible, ego sets about "upgrading" and "renewing" its surroundings by systematically eliminating folkways and structures that inhibit its advance. Relative to ego's overweening ambition, historical precedents for their own sake are "bunk"; traditional authority, an unreasonable restriction; piety, the most significant communal virtue, an empty platitude. After all, ego experiences itself as entirely "self-made," and as owing nothing to anybody. Ego is Ralph Waldo Emerson's hero in "Self Reliance," F. Scott Fitzgerald's self-invented Jay Gatsby, or the pathetic Willy Loman in *Death of a Salesman*.

In community I experience myself solidly anchored in blood and soil, in a shared ground that serves as a reference by which I get my bearings. To be a nomadic ego, in contrast, is to be "homeless."[10] Homelessness is not merely an absence of housing, an easily rectifiable condition. Rather, it is to be uncertain of one's origin and destiny. It is to experience oneself as arbitrarily "thrust" into the life-world, with neither reason nor direction, where instead of being rooted in a place and in a time with purpose and conviction, one floats like an airman.

Homelessness is a precondition for a host of pathologies, not the least of which is anxiety, or as existentialists prefer, angst. Angst is not apprehension about a particular thing such as a growl at night, a shadow in the street, or a specific pain. It is, instead, concern about "nothing in particular." As Heidegger says, "anxiety is anxious in the face of the 'nothing' of the world."[11] It is the alarming sensation of the pettiness, emptiness, irrelevance of ego's existence.

The insomnia, butterflies, hot flashes, and clammy palms symptomatic of angst are decidedly unpleasant. Ego therefore seeks respite in an armory of devices expressly marketed for this very purpose: consciousness-numbing drugs, both illegal and prescribed, and diversions. The latter include listening to talk shows, channel surfing, and general busyness. Ben Franklin, the American paradigm of self-reliance, once composed "A Scheme of Employment for the Twenty-four Hours of a Natural Day." This is the inspiration for today's highly popular "Franklin Planner," a scheduler that encourages nonstop busyness. Among the most commonly recommended activities is, simply, business.

Ennui, Boredom, and Lethargy

Existentialists discern a mood underlying busyness, intoxicant use, and the various other ego-defenses depicted above: ennui, boredom, lethargy. "Ennui" is a particularly revealing French term, meaning literally hatred of one's condition (from *in* + *odio* [hate]). Ego is compulsively on the go for the simple reason that it is profoundly dissatisfied with its present condition. Big Rock Candy Mountain is always just over the next ridge.

Deriving from the Greek *Lethes*, the underground river of amnesia, "lethargy" is equally telling in this respect. Ego keeps "busy as a bee" because it has "forgotten" (or more accurately, never knew) that *This* Is It, to paraphrase a Zen truism. The fulfillment that comes from reconciling to Being is not to be found in the next job, the next marriage, the next town, or the next life. Being displays Itself amidst the very quotidian of everydayness, in things here and now.

ASSOCIATIONS ACCOMPLISHED

As indicated above, the document of an associative relationship is a written contract specifying in detail the responsibilities associates have to each other. Typically, these stipulations are haggled over. Associations may therefore be viewed as "negotiated orders," conversational products, to borrow a phrase from Anselm Strauss.[12] If enemies are constituted by piacular rites, and communities by rites of communion, then a major vehicle for accomplishing associations is the negotiation rite or bargaining routine.

An impressive literature concerning bargaining routines now exists, based on investigations of what transpires daily in schools, factories, clinics, prisons, police stations, and nursing homes. What makes bureaucratic settings particularly amenable to research is that outsiders view their mode of operation as being reducible to statute (book) regulations, formal job descriptions, agency handbooks, and written constitutions. A look behind the scenes quickly reveals the shallowness of this presumption. In every bureaucracy formal regulations are stretched, sidestepped, reinterpreted, and willfully subverted so that the personal interests of their staffs are not compromised. The accommodation of an association's formal structures and strictures to the staff's concerns comprises the "underlife" of an association.[13] As Erving Goffman might say, the underlife testifies to the enduring vigor of the human spirit in the face of what would otherwise encage it, mechanize it, robotize it. A large part of this underlife is bargaining rites.

In the course of work problems arise: A patrolman comes across some kids "cruising the strip" after curfew. How should the case be disposed? In principle, the lawbreakers should be hauled off to juvenile detention. However, if every legal transgression were handled this way before long the entire population would find itself behind bars. Two patients are rushed to a rural hospital with massive heart attacks, but there is only one heart defibrillator. One of the victims is a young professional with three children, the other a retiree. On whom should the machine be used? Still once more, a poor, minority woman under sedation has just delivered an infant many months premature. Should heroic and expensive measures be undertaken to save its life? Maybe she really does not "want" the baby. There are rules against ethnic humor in the office, but we are at war with the Iraqis. Should we post this picture of Saddam Hussein, a bullet hole in his forehead with the caption "Smoke a Camel," to show our patriotism? The examples are endless.[14]

From a distance it appears that police field manuals, hospital procedural guidebooks, state and federal mandates, union contracts, criminal laws, and university bulletins cover all the contingencies faced by bureaucracies. In reality, they rarely do. Sometimes there are no stipulations at all regarding a situation. This happens when new technologies are introduced, ones for which rules have not yet been prescribed. Occasionally, where guidelines do exist they are too vague to be helpful in deciding the proper disposition of the case at hand. Criminal statutes concerning vagrancy, loitering, truancy, public drunkenness, and civil disturbance have this quality. Even those regarding major crimes like rape are notoriously vague.[15] At other times, the guidelines may be clear enough, but they contradict one another, placing people in Kafkaesque role conflicts. Physicians are sworn to do no harm, but also to preserve life. Modern medical technology now enables patients to be placed on virtually permanent life-support, but at risk of imperiling the financial well-being of families and submitting patients to measures bordering on torture. Some regulations are too precise to be applied literally without compromising the association's stated goals. However laudable they may be in other respects, federal accreditation requirements that public schools "mainstream" severely "challenged" pupils take up resources that might otherwise be directed toward educating "normal" children.

Situations like these disrupt office routines and promote animated discussions. Out of these discussions emerge informal operational rules, tacit agreements, work-group standards, and compromises. It is these street-level adjustments, not the formal rules (at least not these alone), that determine what actually transpires on the floor, in the suite, in the classroom, or in the field.

The people involved in negotiating work conditions typically bring conflicting interests to the table. These individuals furthermore, have different amounts of influence they can use to bear on the final outcome. These reflect their respective negotiating skills and the resources they command. The latter include different amounts of skin color, beauty, age, and authoritative credentials. Bargaining resources also include "common sense," notions of what everybody considers to be "realistic" and "reasonable."

To enhance their bargaining positions, skilled negotiators draw upon precedents, customs, and written documents: "We've always done it this way before." "Here's what that rule means in this case." "We tried that earlier and it didn't work." As negotiations proceed there may be dissimulation, participants saying one thing while intending another. A standard ploy is to present one's personal agenda as consonant with those of the association. The reverse of this is to use communal language to disarm one's opponent, as in "Bob, I don't feel like you are really being a team player here; you're thinking only of yourself."

There may be the offering of information, the asking for clarification, outright lies, interruptions, exaggerated claims of one's own importance, posturing: "You need me; I don't need you." "I, at least, am a man of ethics and scruples." Fears may be ventilated; bad motives may be attributed to others; feelings may be hurt; people may be frightened; there may be tensions.[16]

To release stress it is not unusual for humor to be observed during negotiations: the exchange of double-entendres, practical jokes, self-deprecating references. There may even be gestures of touch to mollify concerns. All of these permit momentary distancing from the substantive issues, allowing people to "catch their breath."

More serious breaches of civility may be sanctioned by phrases like, "Al, you're completely out of line." "Sally, I think you're being unfair." If bargaining is to proceed, excuses may have to be tendered, justifications given, or apologies offered. If these are not accepted, reparations may be required in the form of flowers or gifts. Those who continue transgressing the boundaries of decency may eventually find themselves isolated from their peers, and in the most extreme cases exiled from the association altogether. They may, in other words, evolve into enemies in the sense described in chapter 6, scapegoats, objects against whom the others rally and relative to whom they define themselves as "the department," us, the "insiders." Out of associative life, then, can emerge the very feelings of community in principle antithetical to association.

CONCLUDING OBSERVATIONS ON GENERALIZED OTHERNESS

The generalized other is not, as George Herbert Mead seemed to indicate, a single thing. On the contrary, it can be experienced variously as an enemy, a community, or an association: a them, a we, or an it. All three forms of otherness bear on how I experience myself, but each does so differently. Each encourages the disclosure of certain aspects of self, for better or worse, while veiling others, again for better or worse.

Enemies help me delineate who I am by negation, that I am not them. I am not a criminal, a barbarian, a cripple. I am upright and decent, if not perfect, at least normal. By being "thrown apart from me" as diabolic, enemies blind me to the fact that while I may furiously deny it, I too am a repository of death and putrefaction. Death is not just "out there." It also resides in the depths of my own person. Failure to recognize this seemingly simple truth has been a major cause of ordinary "good men" (men and women like you and me) doing the dirty work of mass murder in this century.[17]

I need more than enemies to flourish. I need a home, a home on earth. At best, those without earthly homes are lovable humanoids like E.T. At worst, they become horrifying monsters like The Thing. Regardless of the guise in which they come, as families, religions, gangs, or tribes, communities sate this natural hunger. They give us a heritage, even if partly mythic, a well-trod path to help us through troubled times, and above all, an ego-transcendent reason for living, a *causa sui* infinitely more compelling than career advancement or money making.

Nonetheless, there is a good reason why, from the European Renaissance on, communal existence has come under the criticism of humanists. For if community is a figurative womb, it can also serve as a tomb. As Carl Jung repeatedly shows with the aid of cross-cultural hero legends, human beings must forge personal destinies outside their communities of origin if they are to become fully "individuated." Individuation, as he points out, means more than physical independence.[18] More accurately, it refers to "nondividedness," wholeness, human completeness, wherein one consciously integrates all his or her potential—hence, the significance of associative life. We should never forget that the first modern associations were independent cities, and they were established by contract as refuges from the servile, deadening communal routines of the landed estates. In the city ancient gods would be destroyed, and with them superstitions and worldly powers whose only claim to authority was tradition. With the end of traditional authority arose the modern citizen, the city dweller or burgher, precursor of today's ego.

However this may be, the enthronement of ego has led to a condition visible only in the twentieth century, the impoverishment of Self. Ego-inflation has brought with it a corpus of maladies technically known today as "narcissistic character disorders."[19] As defined by one expert, these are "autoplastic symptoms," including hypersensitivity to slights, delusions of grandeur, rage, envy, reclusiveness, manipulativeness, hypochondria, and depression. The important fact to note about these neuroses is that unless taken to some bloody extreme, as in "going postal" (referring to postal workers gunning down their supervisors), they pass today as the characterology of the average, well-adjusted, successful person.

In sum, then, there can be no "me" without a sense of generalized otherness. Evidently, essential to a fully realized self is engagement with and in a variety of otherness: foes, communities, and associations.

NOTES

1. For a cultural sociology of modern Japanese business practices, see Michio Morishima, *Why Has Japan "Succeeded?" Western Technology and the Japanese Ethos* (London: Cambridge University Press, 1982).

2. William H. Whyte, *The Organization Man* (Garden City, NY: Doubleday-Anchor, 1957), p. 37.

3. Max Weber, *The Theory of Social and Economic Organization*, trans. and intro. A. M. Henderson and Talcott Parsons (New York: Free Press, 1947), p. 337.

4. Ibid., pp. 329–41. Talcott Parsons's first statement, refined in various places, can be found in his *The Social System* (New York: Free Press, 1951), pp. 46–51, 58–67. For a precis of Weber and Parsons, see Roger Jehenson, "A Phenomenological Approach to the Study of the Formal

Organization," in *Phenomenological Sociology*, ed. George Psathas (New York: John Wiley & Sons, 1973), pp. 219–47.

5. For the standard history of existentialism, see William Barrett, *Irrational Man: A Study in Existential Philosophy* (Garden City, NY: Doubleday-Anchor, 1962).

6. Ayn Rand, *The Virtue of Selfishness: A New Concept of Egoism* (New York: Times-Mirror, 1961).

7. For the "church of me," see Robert Bellah et al., *Habits of the Heart: Individualism and Commitment in American Life* (New York: Harper and Row, 1986), pp. 220–21. The "Me Party," a satire of Ayn Rand's political-economic ethics, was observed at the Republican Party National Convention, San Diego, California, July 1996.

8. David Reisman, *The Lonely Crowd* (New Haven, CT: Yale University Press, 1953).

9. Martin Heidegger, *Being and Time*, trans. John Macquarrie and Edward Robinson (New York: Harper and Row, 1962), p. 164. For his portrait of publicness, Heidegger is indebted to Søren Kierkegaard, "The Present Age," trans. Alexander Dru, in *A Kierkegaard Anthology*, ed. Robert Bretall (New York: The Modern Library, 1946), pp. 258–69.

10. Robert Romanyshyn and Brian Whalen, "Depression and the American Dream: The Struggle with Home," in *Pathologies of the Modern Self*, ed. David Michael Levin (New York: New York University Press, 1987), pp. 198–220.

11. Heidegger, *Being and Time*, p. 393.

12. Anselm Strauss, *Negotiation: Varieties, Contexts, Processes and Social Order* (San Francisco, CA: Jossey-Bass, 1978). For a succinct introduction to this concept, see John Hewitt, *Self & Society*, 5th ed. (Boston: Allyn and Bacon, 1991), pp. 236–49.

13. Erving Goffman, *Asylums* (Chicago: Aldine Publishing Co., 1962), pp. 171–320.

14. Factory workers have been told that each weld must be inspected by two independent technicians before proceeding to the next production step. However, there are only four inspectors for 20 welders, each being paid on a piece-work basis. How should they handle this double-bind? Federally funded health clinics are prohibited from providing information on abortion to teen-age girls; or military officers are required anonymously to report suspected homosexual behavior in the barracks to an 800 number. Should these laws be obeyed if obedience means sacrificing one's perceived professional, to say nothing of one's moral, obligations?

For an example of the negotiated accomplishment of the day-to-day routine of welfare agencies, see James Holstein and Gale Miller, "Social Constructionism and Social Problems Work," in *Constructionist Contro-*

versies, ed. James Holstein and Gale Miller (New York: Aldine de Gruyter, 1993), pp. 131–52.

15. William Sanders, "Rape Investigations," in *Sociology of Deviance*, ed. Jack Douglas (Boston: Allyn and Bacon, 1984), pp. 55–64. This book contains other examples of negotiated orders.

16. Erving Goffman, *Interaction Ritual* (Garden City, NY: Doubleday-Anchor, 1967), pp. 97–112.

17. Everett C. Hughes, "Good People and Dirty Work," in *The Sociological Eye: Selected Papers* (New York: Aldine and Atherton, 1971), pp. 87–97.

18. Carl Jung, *The Undiscovered Self*, trans. R.F.C. Hull (New York: Mentor Books, 1957).

19. For one of the early statements on the emerging consensus among psychologists concerning the pathologies peculiar to modern ego, see Ernest Becker, *The Denial of Death* (New York: Free Press, 1973), pp. 176–252. For a more recent anthology addressing the same phenomena, see Levin, *Pathologies of the Modern Self*.

9

EMOTIONS AND THE LIVED-BODY

THE LIVED-BODY

I am more than a talking head. I have a body. There is my body in its physiological-skeletal givenness. Then there is my "body proper" (*le corps propre*), as Maurice Merleau-Ponty honors it, my body as actually experienced or "lived." The first is the preoccupation of biology and modern medicine. This chapter is concerned solely with the second. Its object is to conduct an anatomy of the lived-body and then to speculate on its genesis—so as to destabilize ("destroy") the commonly held belief that the lived-body is organically given.

Merleau-Ponty cites the "phantom limb" phenomenon, wherein amputees sense severed limbs, as proof that bodily experience is not reducible to organic functioning.[1] Lending further credence to his conclusion are pains associated with *no* organic trauma at all—sexual frigidity and impotence among otherwise physiologically fit patients; reports of anorexic females who see themselves as obese; and the documented effects on physical well-being of positive and "negative" placebos such as fake surgeries, sugar pills, and voodoo curses.

We can speculate forever on the reasons behind these observations. Some physiologists attribute them to the existence of neurotransmitters in the cells of the immune system. Human cells, in other words, seem to have "proto-brains." Regardless of the causes, however, they confirm the lived-inseparability of minded-ness and carnality in human flesh. Like the alienation between self and other addressed earlier, the mind/body rift, which is taken for granted as an originary fact, is, according to Merleau-Ponty, a product of psychological (and cultural) development.

Flesh begins bifurcating into mind and body during the course of an infant's exploration of its surroundings. The infant has a memory image of how, with pleasure, it once petted something furry. Now, when it reaches out with a grin to touch a new furry thing, the thing growls and snaps. "This teaches him that his mem-ory images and thoughts are not the same as the world of hard and unpredictable things—that his 'insides' (thoughts) have an ex-istence 'all their own,' which may or may not permit easy control of the outer world."[2]

This lesson is "reified," made more real, when the frightening encounter is labeled. Earlier, the infant had chiseled its mamma and then itself out of the confusion of sensation with words. Now, armed with terms like "thought," "idea," and "wish," it begins to grasp the existence of its own mind-stuff apart from its visible body.

There comes a time when the child is made aware of how its body not only can *receive* signals from furry things, but it can also convey them. That is, its body can be approached like other ob-jects, as something separate from its "self." Its appetites and effusions can be regimented to accord with adult tastes and schedules; it can be molded, adorned, and moved to please adult sensibilities; it can be used to dissimulate and send false messages about what the child really thinks and feels.

While in these respects the child realizes that its body is essential for negotiating the world, it also knows that the child itself is not the same thing *as* its body. "My body is my 'house,'" the child might say, "but not the real 'me.'" In the event of a debilitating injury or terminal illness, the child may be able to retain its self-identity (albeit with probable difficulty). If it has acquired concepts like "soul" and "spirit," it may be capable of imagining that even as its body decomposes, its "true self" will live on eternally. If phantom limbs, chronic nonorganic pains, sexual dysfunctions, and self-starvation can be taken as evidence of a primordial fusion of consciousness with carnality, then what is to be made of reports of out-of-body experiences, wherein consciousness migrates from the body altogether?

However this last question is answered, what needs to be emphasized here is that for the most part in everyday life I am "in my body," not hovering above it in mystical reverie. I do not have to think in order to breathe, to keep my heart pulsing, to walk, or to digest my food. My body becomes discernible as a separate entity only when its functions lose their reliability or when it becomes the occasion of extraordinary feelings: moods, emotions, pains, and pleasures. In this and the following two chapters I deal with each of these things.

MOODS AND EMOTIONS

Popular opinion considers moodiness and emotionality as contrary to rational knowing. "Emotion . . . is . . . an illness of mind," insists a famous proponent of such a view. This is "because . . . emotion . . . exclude[s] the sovereignty of reason." "Emotion," he continues, "is like an intoxicant which one has to sleep off, although it is still followed by a headache." Therefore, "the principle of apathy . . . that the prudent man must at no time be in a state of emotion, *not even in that of sympathy with the woes of his best friend*, is an entirely correct and sublime moral precept."[3]

Max Scheler would disagree. Far from impeding our capacity to know the world and adjust effectively to it, he argues that feelings are our species' most fundamental means of reality orientation. Ed's shrill objections to homosexual marriage scare Bob and disgust him. Not only would it be irrational for him to ignore or suppress his feelings, it could be perilous. For months Alice has repressed her initial inclination to express her outrage at Mary's intimidation of the new office girl. Alice has been taught that hatred is a feeling contrary to a person of her faith. Now, however, she finds herself in the doctor's office diagnosed with what he calls *globus hystericus*, a lump in the throat that cannot be dislodged. At one time, the doctor tells her, this condition was thought to be caused by the swallowing of too many tears. Today, it is explained as a stress-related condition exhibited by those who have been taught to deny the prompting of their feelings.

Emotion-Words

Apprehension, gloominess, despair, and boredom, then, are neither impediments to cognition nor embellishments added to it after the fact. Moods and emotions *are* forms of knowing in their own right. They are "melodies" that reveal how I am "attuned" to my surroundings.[4] As Scheler might say, just as we can know others' minds empathetically (via our heads), we can also know them (occasionally better) sympathetically, through our hearts.

Furthermore, what is born in the heart may well end up in the head, for feelings are often spurs to conscious thought. If the "notes" of my feelings are too discordant or their "rhythms" disrupt my routines, I will be driven to find out what it is I feel and why. In doing so, I may go to friends, to self-help books, or, if these do not help, to experts certified in issuing pronouncements about the body: hypnotherapists, medical doctors, shamans. Provisioned with Adlerian words, Confucian words, Native American words, with the terminology of Vedic healing, and so forth, they may help me get a grip on things, to grasp what it is I feel, and thus to "harmonize" myself to the situation.

The names I give to my feelings reflect situational cues. Thus, my excitability and jumpiness (due to adrenaline) may be labeled in one situation as "anger," in another as "dread," and in still another as "awe." This possibility was first demonstrated in an experiment conducted by Stanley Schacter and David Singer.[5]

After first injecting their subjects with adrenaline to give them comparable sensations, Schacter and Singer assigned half of them to complete a task with a "happy" confederate, the remainder were to do the same with an "angry" confederate. As predicted, when each cohort reported his or her feelings, those from the happy setting described themselves as having been gleeful, elated, or content. Their counterparts depicted themselves as having been irritated, annoyed, or hostile. The same physiological sensations, when given different meanings, produce diametrically opposed emotions.

The significance of this can hardly be exaggerated, for among other things it implies that an emotion or a mood pivotal to one historical epoch or in one culture may be marginal, or entirely absent, in another. It all boils down to the locally advertised vocabularies of emotion and mood.

Max Weber describes the difficulties faced by nineteenth-century missionaries in converting the Chinese to Christianity. While the Chinese understood the concept of shame, they could never quite grasp the meaning of original sin: absolute, unredeemable guilt. Guilt in the Christian sense was considered "undignified" to the Confucian followers, says Weber. Having no emotional appreciation of guilt, the Chinese could hardly be expected to apprehend its complement, being "born-again" in Christ. At most what the Confucian adept might aspire to was a state of quiescent harmony with his or her surroundings, moderation in all things, dignity. Salvation was not only unseemly, it was superfluous.[6]

Emotion-Work

Moods and emotions are paradoxical. On the one hand they can seize and overwhelm us unexpectedly. Lecturing to undergraduates on a father's obligations to his son, Professor Kaufmann's voice suddenly catches in recollection of a fishing trip with his own, now-deceased father three decades earlier. When listening to a mother tearfully beg for the public's help in locating her kidnapped child, I find my own eyes watering and my sense of indignation rising.

Moods and emotions are not just suffered passively; they are also acted out. "Emotion," after all, comes from the Latin (*ex* = out + *movere* = to move); "mood" from the Middle English *mode*, meaning manner of acting. Emotional expression (or mood acting) can be anything from a hang-dog look coupled with a barely audible sigh to a frothing scream of rage. In either case, how I "move out" is bound up with my understanding of the emotional display rules incumbent upon the situation, given who I am.

As to the source of such rules, it is enough to point to emotional style setters: actors, athletes, and musicians. From positions of celebrity they dictate not only clothing fashions, recreation standards, and culinary tastes, but also "in" ways of emoting. Popular mood guides are not always drawn from expected places. Tom Wolfe describes how those in elite circles occasionally spend small fortunes to acquire the dance steps and costumery—which is to say, the moods—of the very people to whom they deny access to their gated communities.[7] The French call it *nostalgie de la boué*, literally, romanticization of mud, the yearning if not to *be* from the lower orders, at least to take on the trappings of their differences—their alienation, hostility, and hopelessness—so as to dramatize one's own significance.

Whatever their final sources, it is not uncommon for emotional mimicry or moods to become so stylized as to provide the basis for literary stereotypes. There is the Russian peasant described by Mikhail Sholokhov who, like the cattle he lives with, plods along, dull witted and stooped, sullenly obedient. There is the Italian *paterfamilias*, arms gesticulating wildly in the course of an afternoon spat in the town plaza; the Samurai whose visage betrays no hint of feeling even in the most provocative circumstances; Nathaniel Hawthorne's righteously grim-faced Puritan minister; the fawning undertaker; the perky cheerleader; her long-suffering, yet beaming mother; the intensely restrained eroticism of Jane Austen's Emma; Gustave Flaubert's *amouress*, her movements voluptuously languid: bold in glance, unrestrained in tongue, contemptuous of Victorian norms of emotional civility. All of these occupy prominent positions in folklore.

"Emotion-work" refers to efforts undertaken to abide by emotional standards; it may be either "shallow" or "deep."[8] Shallow emoting controls the outward gestures, while leaving one's deeper feelings intact. The exhausted and harried airline stewardess loathes the customer in seat 30A with his insistent, whining demands. Yet she disciplines her desire to slap him and continues to smile. As draining as it might be, this is emotional labor at a "superficial" level. Funeral-goers and revival meeting attendees, however, not only wish to ape the gestures of mourning or of being saved, they want to know the sadness of loss and the joy of being found. By intently ridding themselves of distractions and focusing on their task, they call out in themselves the desired feelings. This is "deep" emotional labor.

Arlie Hochschild has itemized some of the tactics utilized today for "psyching ourselves up," "quashing our anger," "having a good time," and so forth. These include recalling past situations where the desired feeling occurred and then reimagining it in the present, technically known as method acting. Another perennially popular aid in the tool chest of the emotional laborer is the mood-altering drug: alcohol, Valium, Ritalin, Librax, Prozac, Darvon, Elevil, Zoloft. For those who have, perhaps, been too successful in controlling their emotions and can now feel "nothing," there also exist therapies directed to "recovering" this part of themselves: Erhard Seminar Training, Primal Scream Therapy, Gestalt, and Assertiveness Training. Emotion-work is not just a sideline in modern society; it is a major industry.

Emotions and moods, then, are more than just feelings; they are also linguistic constructs, and even more than this—actions. Nonetheless, beneath the words and expressions still lie those very feelings. Some are bitter, some are sweet. What makes one sensation a pleasure, another a pain? Let us now turn to this question.

NOTES

1. Maurice Merleau-Ponty, *Phenomenology of Perception*, trans. C. Smith (Atlantic Highlands, NJ: Humanities Press, 1962), pp. 81–82.

2. Ernest Becker, *The Structure of Evil* (New York: Free Press, 1968), p. 124.

3. Immanuel Kant, *Anthropologie*, 73.155–75.158, quoted in Robin May Schott, *Cognition and Eros: A Critique of the Kantian Paradigm* (Boston: Beacon Press, 1988), p. 106. My emphasis. See pp. 137–47 for consideration of the ethical implications of Kant's admonition.

4. Martin Heidegger, *Gesamtausgabe*, vol. 29/30, p. 101, quoted in Michael Zimmerman, *Heidegger's Confrontation with Modernity* (Bloomington: Indiana University Press, 1990), p. 141. Cf. pp. 114–16.

5. Stanley Schacter and David Singer, "Cognitive, Social and Physiological Determinants of Emotional State," *Psychological Review* 69 (1962): 379–99. See also Klaus Scherer, "Relating Situation Evaluation to Emotion Differentiation," in *Facets of Emotion: Recent Research*, ed. Klaus Scherer (Hillsdale, NJ: Lawrence Erlbaum Associates, 1988), pp. 61–77.

6. Max Weber, *The Religion of China: Confucianism and Taoism*, trans. Hans Gerth (New York: Macmillan, 1951), pp. 228–29.

7. Thomas Wolfe, *Radical Chic & Mau-Mauing the Flak-Catchers* (New York: Farrar, Straus and Giroux, 1970).

8. The term "emotion work" was coined by Arlie Hochschild in *The Managed Heart: The Commercialization of Emotion* (Berkeley: University of California Press, 1983), pp. 35–55.

10

PAIN

Neither pain nor pleasure is simply a matter of nerves and neurotransmitters. On the contrary, "we experience pain [and pleasure] only and entirely as we interpret it."[1] Indeed, occasionally the delivery and reception of "pain" may be taken *as* pleasure. Think of the blood-spattered rending of a mother's body in childbirth: in one culture it is counted as a punishment from God; in another the height of orgiastic fulfillment. "Feel the burn," Jane Fonda enthusiastically enjoins viewers of her exercise video, as the sting of lactic acid invades fatiguing muscles; think of the oddly exhilarating emptiness accompanying diets or fasts.

For centuries Christianity has extolled the "delicious wounds," "intolerable joys," and "sweet pains" of self-denial, even to the point of death. Love (Cupid), as it is said, always comes armed with a bow and arrow. This why Plato can declaim, "how wonderful is [pleasure's] relation to pain, which [common sense] supposes to be its opposite." For if one pursues one of the pair, "he is almost compelled to catch the other, too."[2]

Pain and pleasure can both be "worked" like emotions and moods, shallowly or deeply. The first refers to control over the outward cues that conventionally signal their presence: grimaces, tears, "ahhs," and "umms." The second stands for efforts undertaken to mask or to elevate sensations by means of analgesics, nerve blocks, meditation, or biofeedback. Just as emotional labor is undertaken to abide by culturally bound emotion-rules, so are productions of pain and pleasure. Every society is richly endowed with defamatory labels for those who transgress these rules: "crybaby," "wimp," "hypochondriac," "malingerer," "nympho," "slut," "cold fish," "anal personality type." It probably reveals something about ourselves as a people that the Anglo-American thesaurus has far more synonyms for feeling *too much* pain and pleasure than it has for feeling too little. Not only are middle-class Americans discouraged from being, as mother might disgustedly say, "*so* dramatic" or "*so* sensational" in our pleasure/pain displays, but we sometimes find it difficult to identify our sensations in these terms. Persistent adult deviants who fail to "seek appropriate professional help" for transgressing the taboo against exuberance risk being excluded from decent company.[3]

Pain is "anchored in the body," but labors "under the dominion of the mind."[4] This being so, it can appear without any tissue damage at all, as in the torments of couvade (sympathetic labor) or in Benign Intractable Chronic Pain Syndrome (BICPS). Furthermore, as cases like the legendary "human pincushion" illustrate, tissue rending by itself may be insufficient to register painfully, if the mind will not allow it. Even where pain *can be* associated with visible wounds, being mind related it remains maddeningly elusive. One thing is known for certain: lived-pain is not one dimensional, but elaborate and multifaceted. It varies by location, "meaningfulness" ("why me?"), intensity, duration, and by its anticipated implications. "Will I ever be able to work again?" "Is my running career over?" In addition to this, there are different qualities of pain. It can ache, sear, sting, flicker, throb, stab, shoot, and so forth.[5] Most important, lived-pain varies according to its supposed "etiology" or cause. Pain is one thing if it is believed to be the consequence of an accident, something else if it results from your intention to hurt me.

SIN VERSUS SICKNESS

The "medicalization of pain" refers to how allopathic doctors (M.D.s) have assumed jurisdiction over pain in our era—this in the face of widespread skepticism and fear. As Paul Starr tells it, the allopathic hegemony over pain is traceable to its tactical deployment of three rhetorics of well-doing. First, allopaths advertise themselves as guided by humanitarianism and good will, in contrast to the allegedly more mercenary motivations of "quacks"—chiropractics, naturopaths, and homeopaths. Second, it utilizes a scientific approach to diagnosis and treatment, compared to priestly "hocus-pocus." (Allopathic medicine reduces the animated human corpus to a spiritless organism. It dissects it, peers into its cavities, handles its parts, and gazes on its fluids—all in an attitude of scientific detachment.) Third, there is a rhetoric of instrumentation: the use of electronics, rubberized hydraulics, glassware, white enamel, and stainless steel, instead of the candles, chants, robes, and herbs of alternative healers.[6]

In the Age of Faith, as it is called, the Middle Ages (ca. AD 600–1500), pain was seen as a consequence of one's own sins, a condition for which the sufferer himself or herself was held responsible. Each of the seven deadly vices was associated with a characteristic malady: angina with vanity, frenzy with wrath, epilepsy with lust, leprosy with envy, and so forth.[7] Modern pain, by contrast, is attributed to biological abnormalities, that is, to energy imbalances, fluid blockages, or to malfunctioning nerves: deviations from scientifically certified standards of organic functioning. These in turn are attributed to the invasion of the body by one or more foreign substances: bacteria, viruses, fungi, parasites, prions, subatomic particles, and so forth. As such, modern pain is not something for which the victim ordinarily can or rightfully should be held responsible.

The languages of sin and sickness are not simply different lexicons referring to the same thing. The very quale of pain, how pain is "lived," how it is experienced as an entity, depends on the vocabulary used to inscribe it. Those who understand their discomforts as a sign of their own moral turpitude suffer one kind of pain. They beseech God for reconciliation, go to church, confess, and find relief in penance. Sicknesses, on the other hand, are not moral wrongs; they are organic conditions to be "diagnosed" and "remedied."

This being said, there nonetheless exists a fascinating, largely unexplored intersection between the worlds of sin and sickness. For whether conducted under the auspices of clinic or church, the alleviation of pain always entails two events: ritual discourse on the pain itself and the ritual administration of further pain.

Discourse on Pain

Recall that one requirement of medieval penance (chapter 4) was that confessors articulate their missteps to a priest in all the details of their circumstance. Michel Foucault claims that the modern clinical session is little more than a sanitized version of this rite, the original oral narratives having become today's scientific archives.[8] This is not entirely surprising given that sacramental penance itself is believed to have been inherited by the Church from Greek medicine (via Celtic monks).[9] This is the likely source of the idea that the point of penance was not to secure punishment as such, but to "cure the soul" (*cura animarum*). This was supposedly accomplished by the "spiritual physician," as he was called, the priest, prescribing *fomenta* (poultices) to those who had made known to him their "wounds." St. Columban said that just as "physicians of bodies prepare their remedies in various sorts . . . so therefore the spiritual physician ought heal with various sorts of treatments the sorrows, sicknesses and infirmities of the soul."[10]

The parallel of penance to the modern medical, particularly psychiatric, dossier should be evident.[11] In psychiatry too the patient is admonished to set forth the particulars of his or her fantasies, longings, and intentions to a sympathetic, licensed auditor. Like the spiritual confessor of old, the modern physician is trained to uncover inconsistences in what he or she hears, to attend to veiled deceptions, and to disclose "repressed memories"—all to encourage self-awareness and hasten the catharsis of healing. "For if one who is ill is ashamed to make known his wound to the physician," say the ancient penitential handbooks, "it can not be healed."[12]

Pain as Cure

Allusions to the mercies of sympathetic treatment notwithstanding, the "ointments" prescribed for sin in the Middle Ages were anything but tender.[13] This is a second, even more telling, likeness of sin to sickness. Among other tortures, the *medicamenta* for sin varied from hours-long psalm recitations to sleep inhibition by immersion in freezing water, reclining on nettles, being placed in a grave with a corpse, flagellation, fasting, solitary confinement, and years-long exile. The theory behind such practices was that opposites (sins) are best fought with opposites, contraries with contraries (*contraria contrariis sanantur*). This is also, as its title implies, the fundamental axiom of allopathic medicine. With allowances for exaggeration, allopathy handles "contraries" (sicknesses) by utilizing the torments of surgery, intoxication, and irradiation—by cutting, poisoning, and burning recalcitrant flesh. In the case of mental infirmities this means frontal lobotomies, psychotropic drugs, and electroshock.

The notion that pain is best handled by the administration of further pain originates in Greek medicine and in the theory that health involves a kind of arithmetic mean between hot and cold, dry and moist, sweet and bitter, and so forth—hence, pain's curative function: it reestablishes the patient's holistic balance. Just as severe moral infirmities call for extreme *medicamenta*, deadly ailments of the body require their own radical interventions. This is why, until the discovery of anesthesia and antiseptics in the 1800s, the general public avoided allopaths altogether in favor of the more congenial, and often equally effective, prescriptions of homeopaths and herbal healers.

DISEASE VERSUS ILLNESS

"Disease" refers to a pathology of the skeletal-physiological organism, "illness" to a condition of the lived-body.[14] It means not feeling well or not being considered well by biomedical authorities. Diseases are described in terms of lesions, low blood cell counts, bone traumata, and erratic brain waves. The description of an illness, on the other hand, particularly a chronic illness, entails consideration of self-diminishment (due to limb loss, disfigurement, incontinence, etc.); obsessive concern with the latest information about the illness coupled with a tactical avoidance of bad news; rage at one's enfeeblement and at being humiliatingly dependent on others who seem so cheerily well; isolation, confusion, and fear of the future.[15] Biomedicine is wonderfully adept at handling diseases, especially those that are acute, infectious, and life threatening. It is far less able to deal with lived-illnesses.

To be sure, there is considerable overlap between disease and illness. It is also true that one may be terminally diseased, yet feel comparatively "well," and hence *be* well for all practical (phenomenological) purposes. After all, who among us is not organically "dying" at this very moment? The "silent killer" atherosclerosis, HIV, and most cancers in their early stages may be eating at our bodies at the very moment we feel "healthy as a horse"; or vice versa, one may feel or be adjudged "sick," yet be entirely disease free. A case in point is the mental illnesses, or as they used to be known, "psychical pathologies." These are moods and behaviors unsettling to daily routines, but which nonetheless have no evident physiological or neurological causes. Included among them are Attention Deficit Disorder (ADD), Post-Traumatic Stress Syndrome, homosexuality, and addiction, the last two of which are addressed in the next chapter.[16] This category also encompasses what Victorians obliquely referred to as "ladies' conditions."

Ladies' Conditions

With the advent of industrialization, European and American gynecologists begin reporting a host of "nervous fevers" being suffered by their well-to-do clients, "ladies." Cataloged under the title "hysterias," they were said to be exhibited by patients whose "natural function" was not being fulfilled, and whose wombs [*hysterae*] therefore "grieved." Symptoms included melancholy, "erotomania," phantom pains, fatigue, and "andromania" (attributed to suffragists "desirous of being men"). "Terrible state!" concluded one period doctor. "This is the torment of . . . effeminate souls whom inaction has plunged into . . . sensuality."[17] If the preferred remedies of marriage and childbearing were deemed impractical, Victorian medical procedure called for "killing the woman in the woman"—this either by cauterizing the clitoris with acids and white-hot instruments, or by radical hysterectomy, complete removal of the uterus.[18]

During the Age of Faith female flesh was viewed as the paramount occasion for sin. Responsibility for its regimentation fell to the Church in the person of male priests. Stubborn females were disciplined through penance. If unattractive and isolated to boot, they were at risk of being condemned for witchery. Our's, however, is a Medical Age, an era of scientific enlightenment. Gone are superstitions about Woman as the devil's consort. Instead, more typically, She is viewed as "sick."[19] Thus, menopause—until 1940 a natural (and not entirely unpleasant) sign of aging—has become Estrogen Depletion Disease (EDD), a potentially deadly malady calling for "hormone replacement therapy"; premenstrual moodiness and cramping has transmogrified into Late Luteal Phase Dysphoric Disorder (LLPDD); spending too much time before the mirror, a neurosis known as Body Dismorphic Disorder (BDD).[20] Whether vice-laden or abnormal, femaleness, redolent with earthiness, remains problematic, a "pain" (a punishment) requiring further pain.

CONCLUSION

In the world-picture of biomedicine, "health," anciently understood as a state of physical-spiritual wholeness, is reconfigured into a condition of sound glandular-plasmic functioning; "diet," a term originally referring to one's entire way of life, is equated to the organism's nutrient intake; "death" is operationalized as a flat line on an oscilloscope. In short, during the Age of Biology human flesh loses its soul; the body is severed from the mind.

Now pleasure becomes biologized. For the Greeks Pleasure was the child issuing from the marriage of Psyche to Amor, the soul and love.[21] Today, it is understood as a function of dopamine and serotonin levels in the blood. It is an electrical/chemical event produced, most notably, by the "bring[ing] of one's genitals into contact with someone of the opposite sex,"[22] a fleeting excitation of nerve tissue, the orgasm. How this has come to be is the concern of the next chapter.

NOTES

1. These quotes, respectively, are found in David Morris, *The Culture of Pain* (Berkeley: University of California Press, 1991), pp. 2, 29.

2. Plato, "Phaedo," in *Great Dialogues of Plato*, trans. W.H.D. Rouse (New York: Mentor Books, 1956), p. 463. See also Plato, *Philebus & Epinomis*, trans. and intro. by A. E. Taylor (London: Dawsons and Pall Mall, 1972), respectively secs. 46–50.

3. Alfred Lindesmith, Anselm Strauss, and Norman Denzin, *Social Psychology*, 6th ed. (Englewood Cliffs, NJ: Prentice-Hall, 1988), pp. 344–45.

4. Morris, *The Culture of Pain*, pp. 152–60.

5. For the McGill-Melzack Pain Questionnaire, see Morris, *The Culture of Pain*, p. 17.

6. Paul Starr, *The Transformation of American Medicine* (New York: Basic Books, 1982); hence, the plaintive cry of Karl Menninger in his *Whatever Became of Sin?* (New York: Hawthorn Books, 1973).

7. Morton Bloomfield, *The Seven Deadly Sins* (East Lansing: Michigan State University Press, 1952), p. 373. For an updated version of this same idea, see Caroline Myss, *The Anatomy of the Spirit* (New York: Three Rivers Press, 1996).

8. Michel Foucault, *The History of Sexuality*, 3 vols., trans. Robert Hurley (New York: Pantheon, 1978), 1:68.

9. John T. McNeill, "Medicine for Sin as Prescribed in the Penitentials," *Church History* 1 (1932): 14–26.

10. "The Penitential of Columban," in *Medieval Handbooks of Penance*, trans., ed., and intro. John T. McNeill and Helena M. Gamer (New York: Columbia University Press, 1938), secs. A-12, B.

11. Thomas Szasz has drawn a further connection between the Church Inquisition and the modern court-ordered psychiatric hearing. See his *The Manufacture of Madness* (New York: Dell Publishing Co., Inc., 1970), pp. 60–67.

12. Heinrich Denzinger, *The Sources of Catholic Dogma*, trans. Roy Deferari (St. Louis, MO: Herder Book Co., 1957), from the decree of the Fourth Lateran Council, p. 173, sec. 437. See also pp. 274–79, secs. 879–906.

13. See McNeill and Gamer, *Medieval Handbooks of Penance*.

14. Arthur Kleinman, *The Illness Narratives: Suffering, Healing and the Human Condition* (New York: Basic Books, 1988), pp. 3–6.

15. Peter Conrad, "The Experience of Illness: Recent and New Directions," *Research in the Sociology of Health Care* 6 (1987): 1–31; Kathy Charmaz, "Loss of Self: A Fundamental Form of Suffering in the Chronically Ill," *Sociology of Health and Illness* 5 (1983): 168–95; and Rose Weitz, "Uncertainty and the Lives of Persons with AIDS," in *The Sociology of Health & Illness*, ed. Peter Conrad and Rochelle Kern, 4th ed. (New York: St. Martin's Press, 1994), pp. 138–49.

16. See Gerald M. Erchak and Richard Rosenfeld, "Learning Disabilities, Dyslexia, and the Medicalization of the Classroom," *Images of Issues*, ed. Joel Best (Hawthorne, NY: Aldine de Gruyter, 1989), pp. 79–

98; and Stephen Pfohl, "The Discovery of Child Abuse," *Social Problems* 24 (1977): 310–23.

17. Louis-Sebastien Mercier, *Tableau de Paris*, quoted in Michel Foucault, *Madness and Civilization*, trans. Richard Howard (New York: Random House, 1965), p. 157.

18. Barbara Erenreich and Deirdre English, *Complaints and Disorders: The Sexual Politics of Sickness* (Old Westbury, NY: Feminist Press, 1973), pp. 32–35, 38–44. See also Szasz, *The Manufacture of Madness*, pp. 190–92.

19. Foucault, *Madness and Civilization*, pp. 154–57.

20. Peter Freund and Meredith McGuire, *Health, Illness and the Social Body*, 2d ed. (Englewood Cliffs, NJ: Prentice-Hall, 1995), pp. 197–99; Anne E. Figert, *Women and the Ownership of PMS: The Structuring of a Psychiatric Disorder* (Hawthorne, NY: Aldine de Gruyter, 1996); Susan Bell, "Changing Ideas: The Medicalization of Menopause," in *The Meanings of Menopause*, ed. R. Rormanek (Hillsdale, NJ: Analytic Press, 1990); Katherine Phillips, *The Broken Mirror* (New York: Oxford University Press, 1996).

21. Apuleius, *Amor and Psyche: The Psychic Development of the Female*, trans. Ralph Manheim, commentary by Erich Neumann (Princeton, NJ: Princeton University Press, 1956).

22. Herbert Marcuse, *Eros and Civilization* (Boston, MA: Beacon Press, 1955), p. 166.

11

PLEASURE

Pleasure is the satisfaction of desire, the harmonizing of what *should be* with what *is*. What "should be"? What is desire? Infants have neurological impulses; if these go unmet they squirm and squall. However, an impulse is not a desire, and its fulfillment, strictly speaking, is not a pleasure.[1] An impulse is merely a generalized, undirected surge of energy. "Desire," by contrast, is related to the word "consider," which implies a capacity to examine situations so as to choose the best course of action. A desire, in other words, is energy directed more or less consciously toward a concrete end or purpose. Desires have objects. Being without words, infants have no objects, let alone objects for their impulses. These arise as the infant is absorbed by the life-world into which it is born. All life-worlds demarcate zones of licit and illicit desire. What varies are their boundaries. The following sketches seek to destabilize the conviction that the pleasure zones of our inherited world—particularly those concerning sexuality and consumption— are naturally, organically given.

GREEK *APHRODEZIEN*

Aphrodite was patroness of pleasure for the ancient Greeks; her works were *aphrodezien*. Aphrodesia encompassed the entire world of Greek sensual delights: eating, drinking and vomiting, sleeping, massage, bathing, music, and aromas. It also included those pleasures issuing from the "heat of the gymnasium" and from eroticism proper—the touch of one's own body, that of women, boys, girls, and slaves.

Whereas in the modern life-world pleasure tends to be reduced to sexuality (as seen later), Greek eroticism was just one of many desires, and not necessarily the most important. Furthermore, the yearning for sexual congress with a person of the opposite gender was not considered diametrically opposed to that for a person of the same sex. What today are called "heterosexual" versus "homosexual" desires were not associated in Greek erotics with different characterologies, genetics, or destinies. Instead, they were but different reflections of a singular craving to be reconciled with Beauty.[2] In other words, ancient Greek eroticism was motile. It was reasonable and proper to love both boys and girls, adult free women, and slaves of both sexes at various times and simultaneously.

The question for the free Greek male was not which *types* of erotic desires, acts, or pleasures were moral, healthy, criminal. This is a preoccupation peculiar to the Christian ethos. All were "natural," all permissible in the right circumstances. Thus, Orpheus "taught the men of Thrace the art/Of making love to boys and showed them that/Such love affairs renewed their early vigour,/The innocence of youth, the flowers of Spring."[3] Instead, the issue of licit/illicit eroticism revolved around the twin axes of action versus passivity and moderation versus excess.[4]

For a free man to assume a soft, yielding, "effeminate" posture vis-à-vis his erotic partner was always morally suspicious. Even more so was overindulgence. Immoderation was not condemned because eros or the pleasures of flesh in its various guises was bad in itself, just the opposite. It was because the pleasures of a libertine were always *less* than those of a man of moderation, and the goal of the arts of aphrodesia, after all, was the enhancement of pleasure. So, it is said, Socrates "took only so much food as he could eat with a keen relish; and to this end, he came to his meals so disposed that the appetite for his meat was the sauce to it. Every kind of drink was agreeable to him, because he never drank unless he was thirsty."[5]

Second, erotic overindulgence—like gluttony and inordinate sleep—could compromise a man's dignity, a virtue essential to his reputation in the polis. To be a man in the Greek sense was to be in active control of one's feelings and desires. Greek schooling (*askesis*) was intended to inculcate such control. Whereas Christian asceticism mortifies the body with an eye to obtaining beatific visions, *askesis* prepared a man to assume his role as a civil participant in the public life of the people. It is in this context that concern over boy love is best understood.

Although boy love (*paiderasthai* = pederasty) was not viewed as unnatural in Greek ethics, nor (as we know from from Pausanias's speech in Plato's "Symposium"[6]) was it merely tolerated, it was surrounded by an elaborate protocol. There were proper ways to bestow and receive gifts, rules regarding intercessors, recommended places for rendezvous, and forms of invitation.[7] All of these betrayed an anxiety in the community concerning pederasty. Again, this was not because "sex with boys" in itself was judged perverted or evil, but because a youngster's dignity and thus his future status was at risk. As an object of desire by an older male, a boy momentarily played a role more suitable for females or slaves. Accordingly, it was important that he not be available for seduction beyond adolescence.[8]

CHRISTIAN PLEASURE

In the Christian world, the morality of sensual pleasures was assessed by its "fruitfulness."[9] Only those acts undertaken for "natural" procreative ends were licit. Unnatural acts were considered species of *sodomia* (from Genesis 19:24), abominations; as such, they required a penance before the perpetrator could be readmitted into the community of faith. Sodomy included adultery, same-sex coitus, rape, bestiality, incest, pederasty, onanism, and acts against the "laws of marriage": withholding one's body from one's spouse, birth control, or carasses and postures that frustrate the proper end of coupling, such as fellatio and anal intercourse.

Although male-on-male sex was *contra natura* and thus hateful to the Lord, calling for its own penitential remedies, it was not a radically different species of illicitness than the others listed above. Indeed, "sodomy," like "buggery," was not understood as a "sex crime" as such, but rather as a term standing for general threats to the social order. "Buggery," for example, comes from the medieval *Bulgarus* (Bulgarian), meaning a devotee of the Eastern-rite Church, hence a heretic, or more generally, an alien.[10] True, the penances prescribed for same-sex unions in particular were brutal, including death by stoning or burning, and dispossesion. This juridical feature was also evident in the laws of all the American colonies, based as they are on the edicts of the Old Testament as interpreted in Canon Law. Moreover, the punishments for other felonies such as childhood disobedience, robbery, lying under oath, arson, masturbation, and so forth were equally severe.[11]

Most significantly, there was no presumption that homosexual sodomites constituted a different species of being than heterosexuals. (Indeed, as will be seen momentarily, the boundary separating homo- from heterosexual was not yet drawn.) Sodomy was an act that is "committed," not a condition "acquired." As Puritan ministers were fond of repeating, even "the holiest man hath as vile and filthy a nature, as the Sodomites."[12] All persons without exception were thought to have "hearts of buggery," "boiling lusts," "infamous passions." That they did not always act on their inclinations had less to do with their inherent character than to their lack of opportunities. To this extent, however much it differed from Greek ethics in attitude, objective, and technique, the Christian orientation toward sodomy was analogous to that of the Greeks toward pederasty.

This is not to say that the medieval Christian and Puritan worlds of pleasure were identical. In the first place, pleasure was not anathema to the medieval Church as it was to the Puritan. The popular agrarian metaphor that one must approach his wife as a farmer would his field, only while she is in "season," and then soberly "sowing" his "seed," found widespread expression only in the Puritan and Perfectionist conventicles. For the Puritans, all enjoyments were craven, all delights suspect, but not equally so. Instead, the medieval idea was that *voluptates* (sensual pleasures) be put in their proper place in the hierarchy of enjoyments. Pleasure should be incidental to the act of coupling, not the purpose for undertaking it.

MODERN SEXUALITY

With the bourgeosification of the laity after 1800, the more burdensome edicts of the Church fell into disrepute and a new way of reordering pleasure emerged. Licit pleasure continued to be determined by right intention, but intentionality was loosened from the procreative requirement. Now it was sufficient that intercourse be motivated by "love."[13] Love is not just a sentiment. It must be "sincere"—preferably bound to marriage (or in anticipation of such) and home. Accordingly, the definitive Victorian wrongs were prostitution and onanism, sex out of the marital context, sex without "romance."

By the 1920s, however, at least in educated middle-class circles, and by the 1960s generally, sexuality has been freed from even this obligation. Sex for the sake of pleasure becomes the prevailing rule. This development is encouraged by the deployment of biomedicine and the "biologizing" of human flesh. Biology shucks the lived-body of its moral-spiritual husk, leaving behind a disenchanted kernal, the organism. As flesh is biologized, pleasure becomes "one-dimensional," to quote Herbert Marcuse.[14] The Sexual Age proper emerges. Sexuality "explodes," "multiplies," "proliferates." "We . . . become a society of 'sex.' "[15]

Under the regime of biomedicine Ovid's *ars erotica* transforms into the laboratory's *scientia sexualis*. Like comparable disciplines it bases its conclusions on observation. Originally content merely to record the sexual testimonies of practitioners, eventually it insists on gazing on the coital act directly: monitoring the blood pressures and nerve impulses of the partners and measuring their organ distensions. On the basis of this data, the science of sex postulates a single, universal instinct: sex (the libido). All personal dreams and unintended acts are interpreted as neurotic indexes of this instinct; religion, law, and art are viewed as its sublime (sublimated) expressions. "Sexual orientation" is elevated to the sine qua non of personal identity. One's sexuality *is* who one essentially is. The science of sex not only describes; it *pre*-scribes. It refixes lines of sexual propriety in biomedical terms, establishing what Jonathan Katz calls "a proper middle class lust."[16]

The medically certified norm of sexual health is identified at first by implication, by the enumeration of its opposites, *ab*normalities,

perversions. Conditions posed in the Christian era as moral deviations are reframed as "genital neuroses" or as "aberrations of
genetic instinct." Each type of *psychopathia sexualis* is named and
cataloged, and its unique quality of sexual pleasure is described
(the more arousing depictions in Latin).[17] There is "auto-
monosexuality" (otherwise known as "masturbatory psychosis"),
"gynecomasty," "presbyophilia," "paraesthia," "koprolagnia" (a
fascination with defecation), "zoophilia," and "sexoesthetic inver-
sion."

The most pivotal of the illnesses, "homosexuality," does not appear in the archives of modern medicine—that is, does not come
into being—until 1862, 30 years prior to its complement.[18] True,
pederasty and sodomy had been in existence for centuries; but the
homosexual is a different reality than the pederast or sodomite.
Technically, it is a person assumed to be suffering from a pathological *medical* condition. In contrast, pederasty is a Greek custom,
sodomy a moral wrong. The ways in which homosexuality, pederasty, and sodomy present themselves to the consciousnesses of
both practitioner and witness in their respective life-worlds are different emotionally, ideationally, and visually.

The pederast may be *embarrassed* for having fawned inordi-
nantly over a youth who has spurned his favors; but at least "in
our country," Pausanias once said, he is not evil for having desired
a seduction. There are, after all, many loves and all in their own
way are natural and good, although not all equally so. The same-
sex sodomite, in contrast, *has* acted contrary to the Natural Law.
Ipso facto he has excommunicated himself from the community of
believers. He is *guilty*. That being said, he is nonetheless like any
other man. It is his acts, not his nature, that distinguish him, and
these only incidentally. For as already pointed out, all people, even
saints, occasionally succumb to sodomy—some to onanism, others
to incest, still others to bestiality. These are merely variant species
of the *same* deadly vice; all sodomies are forgivable if a firm purpose of amendment is made. Consider now the homosexual.

"Homosexual" was not (originally) intended as a noun standing
for a series of same-sex acts. It represents a *person* with an essentially different ("abnormal") character, of which acts are mere
symptoms. Thus one can *be* homosexual, yet remain celibate. True,
some call for tolerating the difference, others for detering it from

acting on its inclinations by imprisonment, castration, or murder.[19] The ethical ramifications of this disagreement should not be slighted. However, all who have fallen under the mystique of biomedicine consent to the essentialness of homosexual difference.

At first, it is thought that homosexuality is a psychosis caused by "manual self-defilation."[20] Later, it is enframed as a neurosis traceable to a domineering mother whose child rearing has resulted in the homosexual being "fixated" at an "infantile" stage of moral development. As such, it should be susceptible to reform by hypnosis, dream analysis, or aversive shock treatement. Still others write of a genetic basis for the difference, and as evidence cite the discovery of a so-called gay brain.[21] The dispute over causality notwithstanding, however, all consent to the notion that homosexuality (like heterosexuality) is a foundation on which rests the entire person: his job preferences, tastes in dress and music, recreations, kinesthetics, verbal and mathematical aptitudes and emotional attitudes, and particularly, desires.[22] This is a far different thing than the Greek pederast or Christian sodomite.

DRUG ADDICTION

Intoxicant use is universal and it persists even where the most severe measures are undertaken to deter it. Although the following anecdote concerns tobacco, analogous tales could be cited for alcohol, opium, coffee, cocaine, tea, marijuana, and peyote, to say nothing of various synthetic drugs.

> Wherever the Sultan [Murad IV, ca. 1650] went on his travels or on a military expedition his halting-places were always distinguished by a terrible increase in the number of executions [for smoking tobacco]. . . . He was fond of surprising men in the act of smoking, when he would punish them by beheading, hanging, quartering, or crushing their hands and feet. . . . Nevertheless, . . . the passion for smoking persisted.[23]

Sociologists theorize that universal and persistent social traits exist because they are "functional." I need not speculate here on what the social functions of intoxication might be. What interests

me is that while permitting, encouraging, and sometimes even sub-
sidizing appetites for some toxins (in America, tobacco and alcohol), every society also designates the use of others as "dangerous,"
"criminal," or "sinful," and embarks on quests to discover their
presumed pathogeneses. As in matters of sexual deviance, these
undertakings are largely arbitrary and will likely fail. For just as
the cause of beef eating is identical to that for eating foods that
are tabooed (e.g., pork; although beef eating among higher-caste
Hindus is itself taboo), or the cause of drinking nonkosher wine is
like that for drinking wine that has been blessed by a rabbi, the
cause of the desire for stigmatized toxins is probably similar to
that for illicit toxins.

The etiology of drug abuse presently holding sway revolves
around the biomedical paradigm of addiction. Two literatures
compete for prominence. The first maintains that some individuals
are prone to drug abuse because they harbor "addictive personal-
ities." This is either because of their genotype (see below) or because they are neurotically obsessive due, among other possibilities,
to toilet-training traumas. The second theory locates the addictive
power of particular drugs in their own chemistries. "You need take
it just once," goes the saying, "and you're hooked." The idea here
is that the body builds a tolerance to certain chemicals so that if
they are taken away the user experiences profound discomfort. The
pleasure of the drug is found in the absence of withdrawal pains.
Addiction, in other words, is a state of biological homeostasis.

This is neither the place to adjudicate the truth of these accounts
nor to offer a substitute. Instead, I want to assume a critical phenomenological stance toward addiction. This involves two steps:
first, I will bracket addiction, rendering it into the word "addiction"; next, I will examine the circumstances of its coinage and
dissemination. Together, these should "destroy" (undermine) the
natural attitude toward the thing, that is, the belief shared by abu-
seologists and the public that addiction has an ontology independent of our consciousness of it—that once discovered and explained,
it can be "controlled."

"Addiction" comes from the Latin (ad [to] + dicere [to say or
pronounce]). In Roman Law it meant the delivery of a person (the
addictus), usually a debtor, into the power of his creditor upon the
utterance of a ritual phrase. This is the basis of the rhetorical power

of the word. To be addicted, metaphorically, is to be "enslaved" to a substance. The task of the abuseologist is to liberate the patient from his or her thralldom. While "addiction" never entirely dropped this ancient Latin resonance, in English it took on additional, more neutral connotations, coming to stand for "being delivered into the power of" any sort of habit, good or bad, as in phrases like, "she's 'addicted' to learning," "he's 'addicted' to running," and so forth.

Alcohol addiction was officially identified as a mental illness for the first time in 1934 by the American Psychiatric Association.[24] Whether or not this date is merely coincidental, it is worth noting that in the year just prior to this the Prohibition amendment was repealed, effectively decriminalizing alcohol use. On first glance the coining of "alcohol addiction" appears to be a classic case of jurisdiction over waywardness being transferred from one body of well-doers (the police) to another (physicians).

In 1935 the American Medical Association confirmed the wisdom of the psychiatric pronoucement, passing a formal resolution declaring alcoholics "valid patients." This was the same year that "Dr. Bob" and Bill Wilson founded Alcoholics Anonymous (AA), the therapeutic prototype for all subsequent addictions: gambling, sex, narcotics, smoking, and so forth.[25] It is ironic that the meeting format described in AA's "The Book" has the aura of a Protestant evangelical revival, consisting of public confessions, vows of abstinence, and admissions of one's powerlessness in the face of his or her appetites. It is doubly ironic that the final step in programs for liberating victims from "enslavement" to personal power involves surrendering to another, unspecified, "higher power."

If debates concerning the proper status of same-sex relationships and obesity are any basis for prediction, there was probably vigorous argument among period health professionals concerning the best way to classify the injestion of deviant substances. Although details of this debate still await examination, its outcome has already been documented.

In medical textbooks published in 1887 mention is made of "chronic intoxication" and "self-administered 'poisoning' " as bona fide medical conditions. Prior to that year, however, there is little record of drunkeness and "opium eating" officially being considered anything other than criminal or religious problems, that is, as issues to be dealt with either by incarceration or by compulsory attendance at temperance education classes. (The latter were instituted nationwide in public schools by 1900.) To cite just one example, the 1883 edition of Kraepelin's classic medical textbook does not mention alcohol use, opium, or cocaine as *medical* concerns. However, 40 years later in 1920, the U.S. Treasury Department published regulations outlining "medical treatment for addiction" under auspices of the Harrison Narcotic Act of 1914. This is the first unambiguous, authoritative acknowledgment of the existence of addiction. Even 20 years after this, in 1940, the standard history of the psychiatric profession makes no reference specifically to addiction as a medical problem.

Due to lobbying efforts by the Yale University Center for Alcohol Studies and the National Council on Alcoholism, the disease theory of addiction found an increasingly favorable audience in the American medical profession after 1940. In brief, this theory asserts that only a specific proportion of inebriates, "gammas," are certifiably addictive; only these should be considered candidates for medical treatment. Gammas are supposedly drinkers with a "sensitivity" or "allergy" to alcohol and thus cannot control their craving for it. Not until 1956 would the American Medical Association formally adopt this idea as it own.

In summary, it can be said that while the precise dates for the creation and dissemination of drug addiction cannot be fixed, given the information available today, it seems to have been christened sometime around 1920, certainly after 1935. However: it only became fully assimilated into the psychiatric medicine chest two decades after that, at the earliest.

The impatient reader will object that whether the ingestion of an intoxicant is interpreted as a sin, a felony, or a sickness is irrelevant. The point is that it is harmful to both consumer and to society and therefore should be banned. For the benefit of still unconvinced skeptics, let me go over it one last time.

A phenomenon is the prototypical experience of a thing: how it is seen, thought, felt, and recalled. How something presents itself to consciousness depends largely on how it is written and spoken, on the words used to enframe it. To "self-poison" oneself by consuming alcohol or opium calls for police intervention and maybe a night cooling out in the drunk tank. To be absolved of "gluttonously indulging" the same substances requires that the penitent undertake a period of prayerful abstinence. "Addiction," on the other hand, necessitates hospitalization under the doting authority of medical professionals and/or participation in a 12–step program with "recovered" victims. True, one may be a felon, a penitent, and a patient all at once, but this does not gainsay the point being made here, namely, that these are three different kinds of things.

Dangerous Drugs

It is unnecessary to spend more than a few sentences on the phenomenological essence of illicit drugs. What needs to be emphasized is that the difference between these and other equally toxic, habit-forming, but legal (occasionally prescribed) substances has less to do with their physical chemistries than with what Thomas Szasz calls their "ceremonial chemistries," their symbolic associations. One of these concerns the drug's source. Other things being equal, those substances that tend to be banned or medically tabooed are readily and cheaply grown and processed, that is, they are not produced and marketed by registered pharmaceutical firms. Heroin is therefore illegal, but its synthetic substitute, methadone, is not; marijuana is illegal, but as a prescribed pharmaceutical, marinol, it is not; cocaine is illegal, but in its medicinal form, novocaine, it is not, and so forth.

According to Szasz, however, the single most important phenomenological attribute of a dangerous drug is its connection to one or more of the minority groups. Virtually every drug condemned at one time or another by American authorities as "addictive" has been mythically tied to the lifestyle of such groups: distilled alcohol (to nineteenth-century Scotch-Irish, Russian, and Italian immigrants), wine (to Jews and Catholics), beer (to Germans), opium (to Chinese laborers), marijuana (to Africans and Hispanics), cocaine (to Hispanics), peyote (to southwestern Indians), and so forth. The execration of the drug, in other words, has been part of a more general defaming of the group in question. Each drug "explains" the ferocity, criminality, sexual excesses, mendacity, stupidity, and laziness alleged to belong to the group to which it is tied by legend. (Analogous connections can be drawn between minority groups and "un-American" clothing fashions and "dangerous" musical styles such as syncopation, jazz, rock-and-roll, and most recently, rap.[26]) In short, in place of attacking the group in question directly by name, majority opinion condemns alleged attributes of its lifestyle and undertakes campaigns to maintain its purity by vaccinating itself against contamination; hence, America's periodic drug wars.

CONCLUSION

Abuseology and the science of sex are just two examples of the biologizing of human flesh in our era. While each addresses a different wayward desire, both begin by supposing that the body is reducible to the organism. Both, in other words, understand deviant pleasure to be an illness. True, the precise disease conditions affecting the illnesses have yet to be determined with certainty: the chromosomal location of the "gay gene," for example, or that of the "gamma gene." Like the search for the genes alleged to cause other deformations of the body politic—depression, eating disorders, classroom misbehavior, poverty, or handgun violence (the list is virtually endless)—there is no doubt among those in the medical profession that they will eventually be found. After all, each of these conditions is known to "run in families."

The appeal of this idea hardly needs stating. For if it is indeed true, then rehabilitation can be accomplished through a series of individualized (insurance underwritten?) medical interventions: surgical gene splicings, drug therapy, and the like. *Voila!* Now social reform becomes possible without having to alter the structures of society.

NOTES

1. C. Wright Mills and Hans Gerth, *Character and Social Structure* (New York: Harcourt, Brace and World, 1953), pp. 44–48.
2. Michel Foucault, *The History of Sexuality*, 3 vol., trans. Robert Hurley (New York: Pantheon, 1978), 2:187–88.
3. Ovid, *Ovid: The Metamorphoses*, trans. Horace Gregory (New York: Viking Press, 1958), book 10, Orpheus and Eurydice.
4. Foucault, *The History of Sexuality*, 2:38–55.

5. Xenophon, *Memorabilia*, trans. J. W. Watson (New York: E. P. Dutton, 1927), book 1, sec. 3, para. 5.

6. "Those who are inspired by this [higher] love turn to the male," says Pausanias. "For they love not boys, but intelligent beings whose reason is beginning to be developed, much about the same time at which their beards begin to grow." "Symposium," in *The Dialogues of Plato*, trans. B. Jowett (New York: Random House, 1937), p. 309. Pausanias goes on to distinguish between "vulgar love" for the youth's body, and a virtuous love for his soul, p. 311.

7. Foucault, *The History of Sexuality*, 2:195–99.

8. Ibid., 2:215–25.

9. Ibid., 1:36–49.

10. Thomas Szasz, *The Manufacture of Madness* (New York: Dell Publishing Co., Inc., 1970), pp. 164–66.

11. Jonathan Katz, "The Age of Sodomitical Sin, 1607–1740," in *Reclaiming Sodom*, ed. Jonathan Goldberg (New York: Routledge, 1994), pp. 47–48.

12. Ibid., p. 52.

13. Jonathan Katz, *The Invention of Heterosexuality* (New York: Penguin Books, 1995), pp. 40–47.

14. Herbert Marcuse, *One-Dimensional Man* (Boston, MA: Beacon Press, 1964), pp. 56–78.

15. Foucault, *The History of Sexuality*, 1:103–8.

16. Katz, *The Invention of Heterosexuality*, pp. 57–82.

17. The classic textbook is Richard Krafft-Ebing, *Psychopathia Sexualis: With Especial Reference to the Anti-Pathic Instinct* (Brooklyn, NY: Physicians and Surgeons Books, 1922 [1892]).

18. Katz, *The Invention of Heterosexuality*, pp. 20–22, 51–54. To simplify affairs, the following discussion concerns only male homosexuality. But see Celia Kitzinger, *The Social Construction of Lesbianism* (Newbury Park, CA: Sage, 1987).

On August 14, 1997, the American Psychological Association passed a resolution requiring members to read to their patients a statement declaring homosexuality normal and healthy. Nonetheless, the medical status of homosexuality is still being contested. My observations deal with the original sense of "homosexuality," as something abnormal and suspect.

19. Richard Plank, *The Pink Triangle: The Nazi War against Homosexuals* (New York: Henry Holt, 1986).

20. For "masturbatory psychosis" and its consequences, see Szasz, *The Manufacture of Madness*, pp. 180–206.

21. For a report on recent discoveries of a possible genetic basis for

homosexuality, see David Nimmons, "Sex and the Brain," *Discover*, March 1994, pp. 64–71.

22. Jeffrey Weeks, "Sexual Identification Is a Strange Thing," *Against Nature: Essays on History, Sexuality and Identity* (London: Rivers Oram Press, 1991), pp. 79–85. See also Amy Bloom, "The Body Lies," *The New Yorker*, 18 July 1994, pp. 38–49, concerning "males" becoming "females," and "females," the reverse. It raises the problematic, and possibly contrived, nature of sexual identity.

23. Quoted in Thomas Szasz, *Ceremonial Chemistry* (Garden City, NY: Doubleday-Anchor, 1975), p. 173.

24. The following history is based on Ibid., pp. 2–17, 177–84.

25. For a comprehensive history of AA and a description of its program by its own founders, see *Alcoholics Anonymous* (New York: Alcoholics Anonymous World Services, Inc., 1976 [1939]).

26. For elaboration on this thesis see Craig Reinarman and Harry G. Levine, "The Crack Attack: Politics and Media in America's Latest Drug Scare," in *Images of Issues*, ed. Joel Best (Hawthorne, NY: Aldine de Gruyter, 1989), pp. 115–38.

12

AN ARCHAEOLOGY OF MODERNITY

All life-worlds are given as coherencies of things, beings that are present, that are there: animate and inanimate entities, natural things, and artificial devices. The modern life-world in particular presents itself to consciousness as a coherency of *objective* things, of objects: material, social, and ideal.

In common discourse "object" and "thing" are conflated. This is understandable in that "object" comes from the Latin *objectum*, meaning that thrown before the senses, hence that which is sensible, nameable, knowable. However, *objectum* also contains a special resonance I want to emphasize here, namely, as an obstacle or hindrance (from *objacere* = to lie against). An object (and an object world) is that which impedes the realization of my goals and which therefore must be overcome if I am to proceed. Either I subdue it, or it me. That Alfred Schutz understands this second sense of "object" is evident when he asserts that "in order to realize our goals, we must master and transform the life world . . . , for these objects offer to our actions a resistance which we must either subdue or to which we must yield."[1] This being said, the only realistic stance to take toward a world of objects (including human objects) is the Will to Power, or as Schutz prefers, "pragmatism."[2] Even Martin Heidegger, who would later advocate artistic "rele-asement" of things to themselves, originally proposed that man's "primordial relation" to the antagonistic power of the world is aggressive. "We uncover nature . . . not through reflection about it, but in struggle with it and fight against it, in *becoming master over it.*"[3]

Objects are "resources," "standing fields," "goods," "opponents" to be owned, ordered, defeated, and made over in man's image and likeness, or in a softer, more comprehensive word, "managed." The disciplines most congenial to this attitude include natural resource management (forestry, agriculture, mining, fish and game, environmental fields, and waste management) and *human* resource management sciences (business, hospital and political administration, military science, corrections and penology, social work, and the health professions). The degree to which the things of the world are cost-effectively subdued is called "progress." Progress is made possible by exact measurement, making objects fall under the calibrated ruler of the sovereign subject.

Modernity ascribes a self-certain ego, radically alienated from the object world (including from other egos) and toward which it assumes a judgmental, militant, grasping stance. Whether garbed in the work pants of the proletariat, the leather walking britches of the Aryan folk, or the power suit of the corporate magnate, ego's taming of the world's objects is lauded in epic literature, monumental art, and music.

When directed outward, ego's Will to Power tames nature and its savage inhabitants. A forest becomes board feet of lumber; a rapids, kilowatts of electricity; hoofed animals, meat stock; the aborigine, a man-power production unit or public relations windfall. When turned inward against ego's own "private wilderness," the Will to Power overcomes the body's temptings by mortifying its flesh. In the event that wildness cannot be defeated or the unforeseen costs of conquest are prohibitive, ego fantasizes fleeing the object world altogether by space craft and rocket (or less dramatically, by simply packing up its car, and leaving the mess behind). All the purported "wonders of the West," from inoculation against disease to extended life spans, from the Green Revolution to the watering of deserts, from urban metroplexes to the Global Village are attributable to ego's dominating spirit.

BEGINNINGS

The archaeology of modernity inquires into how the life-world became an arena for ceaseless progress. It does this by tracing the project of modernity to its generative pronouncements in prophecy and poetry (from *arche* = origin). This requires sifting through layers of sediment and accumulated debris, through institutional practices and barely conscious routines until one can go no deeper: past rectangular architecture and rational chord-progressions; beyond linear-time, the idol of money, and the militarization of workplace, school, and play; past disease-related sicknesses, and biological sexualities; past ego's craving for self-actualization; and finally to their foundational conversations.

Originary words accomplish two things simultaneously.[4] They first disclose, reveal, illuminate Being. Heidegger calls this event *Seinsgeschick* (*Sein* = being + *Geschick* = flashing), "flashing of being." Without words, says Heidegger, Being has no way to display itself, to give itself to us. In the prophetic moment is glimpsed what before was hidden. Now a paradox arises: the words that reveal Being also veil what they disclose. This is the second accomplishment, the negative side, as it were, of prophecy: it represents a closure of Being to those who hear it, understand it, and take it for truth. Like lightning, the "flashing of being" in the dark may be so brilliant as to blind those enraptured by it. The concealing moment of revelation is lost sight of; the word-constructed world is taken *as* Being-itself. World histories become narratives of "falleness," of the forgetting of Being.

As described in chapter 2, new worlds are birthed at the death of the old. In the breakdown of ordinary affairs, a space, a clearing, an opening is made for the "in-flashings" of revelation. Lucifer, the light-bringer, shows himself at night.

The anthropologist Anthony Wallace describes the process.[5] When a people's "mazeway," their traditional way of life, is unable effectively to address new challenges, stress mounts, and "neuroses" then appear: wish-fulfilling dreams, hallucinations, fantasies, and above all, prophecy. Although they should not be considered psychotic in the clinical sense, these "symptoms" are analogous, Wallace insists, to those recorded by inmates of mental institutions.

Bernard Barber agrees. He says the situation facing prophets is "anomie," the shattering of a people's normative order, primarily because of material deprivation.[6] The emergence in the nineteenth-century of the Native American Ghost Dance occurred after the disappearance of the buffalo, which up to that time had served as the economic staple and cultic centerpiece of Plains Indian life. This loss, coupled with the introduction of whiskey by white traders and the decimation of the population by smallpox, destroyed the plausibility of the traditional cosmos. A predictable result followed: a series of prophetic revelations promising a better life with the adoption of a new moral code. Beginning with the Seneca seer Handsome Lake, it culminated in the peyote religion still observed in the Far West.[7]

Martin Luther, John Calvin, Thomas Hobbes, Rene Descartes, and Francis Bacon flourished in the period immediately after AD 1500. As mentioned earlier, all are implicated in the enterprises usually associated with the word "modern": laboratory science, the university, industrial capitalism, Protestantism, state bureaucracy, nationalism, individualism. Most historians believe the ground-words of modernity had already been laid during the course of a centuries-long series of crises in Eurasia during the first millennium BC. Although the details are permanently lost, they were likely occasioned by contact between Mesopotamian, Persian, and Aegean cultures due to war, migration, and trade.

Heidegger on Beginnings

Martin Heidegger gives one account of the story.[8] The site was the agora, the public space, lying at the foot of marble temples in pre-Christian Athens. Here, ongoing debates were conducted concerning the possibility of goodness and truth and thus of legitimate authority. Some took the position that truth and goodness are merely the claims of sophists foisting their own political agendas. Truth, in other words, is relative. Others like Socrates, frightened by what this might mean, argued in favor of the possibility of certain knowledge. The prophetic turn was the move by Plato in the Allegory of the Cave away from *phainomena* toward concern with their essences.[9]

Anciently, *phainomena* were understood to reveal their truth, their being, spontaneously if man awaited their presence in silence (from *phainesthai* = to appear, from *phos* = light). In the Allegory of the Cave, however, *phainomena* were spoken of as mere "appearances," illusions, shadows on the cave wall: things to which lesser men attend. Plato admonished readers to turn their backs on the fleeting apparitions and look toward the cave entrance so as to grasp their essences (*eidos*). This is what makes the appearances possible in the first place.

Informed by a political-military way of looking on worldly affairs, the Romans refined Greek metaphysics, says Heidegger, giving it a twist familiar to modern readers.[10] Truth is not something that freely shows itself, Roman philosophy insisted. Rather, it must be "captured," "apprehended," "grasped" by the power of reason. For the things to be known are objects, as characterized earlier; they resist our attempts to know them. Deciphering them therefore involves setting upon them as one might an enemy, naming them, and giving their reasons for being, their causes, the conditions that produce them. Only in this way can they be brought under man's sway.

Contrast this to the ancient Greek notion of *theoria*, attentive gazing at what is, meditative openness to the presencing of beings. The Latin translation for *theoria* is *contemplari* (contemplation). Although according to Heidegger *contemplari* suggests an attitude of receptivity, in its speculative form it refers to the intellectual activities of dividing, demarcating, classifying, and judging things. In Roman *contemplari*, in other words, the way already surveyed by Plato is cleared for the engines of modern science: from a passive beholding and wondering to an active seizing, a regimenting of things by measurement and causal analysis.

Weber on Beginnings

Modernity is not simply a child of Greek philosophy. In Max Weber's sociology of Occidental consciousness, the Platonic connection goes virtually unmentioned. Instead, he assigns the seminal role to Semitic goatherders and to a lineage of prophets—Moses, Isaiah, Ezekiel, Amos, and so forth—who in praising God belittle the things of the world.[11]

Again, the originary words were spoken in a clearing—not in the enclosed plaza of the Greek polis, but in the desolate expanses of the Negev Desert. There a nomadic tribespeople—honoring themselves after a minor warrior god—had wandered for 40 years. The prophetic moment occurred with an epiphany familiar to those who reside under the limitless vault of the cloudless sky: "Thou art all, I am nought!" It revealed divine transcendence and the relative worthlessness of the world.

God resides in the heavens, magisterial, inscrutable, unapproachable. Nameless, He can never be subjected to human manipulation. Compared to His Being worldly things are "fallen," not sacred but sinful. Mankind itself, while created in God's image, is but dust and ashes, and will return to this condition at death.

Platonic revelation dismisses worldly *phainomena*, self-disclosing appearances, as shadows on the cave wall and unworthy of serious attention. The lover of wisdom is admonished to direct his contemplative gaze to heavenly forms. Now comes the Hebraic insight that the things of this world are not merely illusory and wonder at them is a sign of ignorance, but rather they are *craven* and attachment to them is *idolatrous*, a sin worthy of death.

To be sure, having been fabricated by a Creator each creation is loved, according to St. Augustine, and each in its own way is good: rocks, trees, beasts, mankind. The epigraph of Pope Pius X quoted in the preface to this book, anathemizing "anyone [who] says that . . . God, . . . cannot be known . . . by . . . the things" of the world, reflects traditional Roman Catholic dogma on this point. Even man's failings are but *felices culpae*, happy faults, occasions for the preeminent good, Christ's incarnation. John Calvin, doctor of the Protestantisms that inform the first truly modern cultures, abjured euphemisms. Human beings, he declared, are essentially damned. "There is none that doeth good, no, no one." Even infants "bring their condemnation into the world with them, . . . for though they have not yet produced the fruits of their iniquity, yet they have had the seed of it within them. Their whole nature is . . . a seed of sin and therefore cannot but be odious and abominable to God."[12] The same can be said of the infant's mother: her very title, *mater*, implies materiality; her watery substance ebbs and flows with the lunar cycles of the night. Woman is a failed project of manhood, a gateway to Hell. Even Catholic dogma comports with Calvin on the danger of the female. "Many have perished by the beauty of a woman," said Innocent III.[13] She must either be avoided altogether, or if this is impossible, be approached with objective detachment and made over in a manner pleasing to the Lord: straightened, corrected, made right.

It is out of this theological context that the attitude of scientific aloofness vis-à-vis reality emerges, and the impetus for its unending improvement.[14] Now comes Descartes's "object world," composed of things to be engaged with, fought, and mastered, the world of our inheritance.

First brought under the scrutiny of modern sensibility are the attributes of physical things, their motions, masses, accelerations, and so forth. Seeing success in explaining (and controlling) these, attention turns next to human beings. The behavioral sciences are christened, notably psychology and sociology. True, human activity has always provoked curiosity, but the modern idea is to uncover its causes and so place it under a *scientific* regimen. Again, while the desire to manage moral choices is hardly a new idea, the thought of *engineering* preferred outcomes is.

Some management experts hope that "mankind will be able to find its best meaning as a machine in the service of [the] economy—as a tremendous clockwork, composed of ever smaller, ever more subtly 'adapted' gears."[15] Others believe us to be self-regulating cybernetic systems, effective control of which requires that our "thermostat settings" be altered or the information "feedback" changed. With the rising prestige of biomedicine, however, the prevailing view has come to be that humans are essentially organisms and that disciplining them requires biochemical and genetic interventions. Whether pictured as machine, servo-mechanism, or biomorph the modern person is thought, seen, and spoken of as an object, an obstruction, an unruly entity needing ensnarement in a trap suited to its specifications.

Endings

Life-worlds contain seeds for their demise in the words out of which they come. Prophecy legitimizes the institutional arrangements—the "sedimentary debris" mentioned above—that confute them. These contradictions become evident as worlds bump against each other and against the contingencies of Earth. The founding words of a prophecy are exposed as problematic; they lose credibility; the world fractures along its inherent fault lines and collapses.

The contradictions of Aztecan reality with its pantheon of insatiable gods were disclosed in the course of contact with the Spanish. To provide their gods nourishment in the form of *chalchihuatl*, human blood, for their struggles against the forces of night, the Aztecs conducted "flowery wars" (*xochiyaoyotl*) with their neighbors to harvest human hearts. Hernando Cortez skillfully enlisted these neighbors as allies in his conquest of the capital city of Tenochtitlán.

The pronouncements of Plato and Moses also harbored implications unimaginable when first uttered. Today they have become gruesomely evident in the form of breakdowns, "externalities" as economists call them, of ever more expansive scope: toxic waste and global warming, virulent infections, over-population, total war, the Bomb.

Feelings apprise us of how things are going in the world. Fear and horror in particular tell us of expectations gone awry, that the once reliable habits of perception and tongue no longer work. While most find respite from such feelings in be-drugged unconsciousness or in diversions, it is given to others to be carriers of "in-flashings," ways through the impasse. Some call these latter the "holders of the tension." For them, darkness is the "saving power" (Hölderlin) because it elicits from them new horizons of possibility.

The path of endless struggle with the things of the world with an eye to their total control seems destined to culminate in a dead-end, exterminism.[16] This frightful realization compels tension-holders to rethink matters.

An insight is apparent: *things are not necessarily obstacles to be overcome.* Although they can be pictured this way, it is not required by the things-themselves. Specifically, you as one of those things need not be my antagonist, let alone my enemy—the repository of my own unassimilated garbage, my own lust and violence.

A second insight is revealed: *the worth of things is not given entirely in their utility.* You do not exist merely for my use, not even for the pleasure I take in your beauty, intelligence, or skills. In the final analysis, you are for yourself.

Admittedly, these are hardly ground-shaking revelations; nor for that matter are they particularly new. Immanuel Kant, for one, has articulated an ethics on these same lines. Furthermore, the two injunctions say little about how to engage things. Granted, we are not to view each other merely as use-objects. But how should we be together?

While an exhaustive answer to this question cannot be given here, it seems that at a minimum we must relearn how to treat things for-themselves. We must approach them with reverence and care. This implies nothing less than to deal with them "religiously" (from the Latin infinitive *relegere* = to take care). This is not because they are necessarily nice or pretty, but more to the point because they are ultimately unknowable and mysterious, dark, possibly dangerous.

To relate to people in a religiously guardful, preserving way has definite implications for the ethics of human inquiry, to say nothing of other realms. Specifically, instead of *im*posing theories on their subjects, investigators are admonished to let subjects *dis*close themselves. All of what this might entail goes beyond the concerns of this book. Among other things, however, it may well require that investigators "surrender" openly and flexibly to their subjects. In other words, if they expect their subjects to reveal themselves, investigators may first have to reciprocate the favor in kind.[17] In any case, investigators must begin cultivating a habit of wonderment toward their subjects, not just astonishment at their dramatic and scandalous side—which is to say, the newsworthy and novel, hence the minor—but toward their very ordinariness.

NOTES

1. Alfred Schutz and Thomas Luckmann, *The Structures of the Life-World*, trans. Richard M. Zaner and H. Tristam Engelhardt, Jr. (Evanston, IL: Northwestern University Press, 1973), p. 6. Again, "the life world is something to be mastered according to my particular interests. I project my own plans into the life world, and it resists the realization of my goals," p. 15.

2. Friedrich Nietzsche, *The Will to Power*, trans. Walter Kaufmann and R. J. Hollingdale (New York: Vintage Books, 1968).

3. Martin Heidegger, *Phanomenologische Interpretation von Kants Kritik der reinen Vernunft*, p. 21, quoted in Michael Zimmerman, *Heidegger's Confrontation with Modernity* (Bloomington: Indiana University Press, 1990), p. 162. Zimmerman's emphasis.

4. Martin Heidegger, *The Question of Technology and Other Essays*, trans. and intro. William Lovitt (New York: Harper and Row, 1977), pp. 36–49.

5. Anthony Wallace, "Revitalization Movements," *American Anthropologist* 58 (1956): 264–81.

6. Bernard Barber, "Acculturation and Messianic Movements," *American Sociological Review* 6 (October 1941): 663–69.

7. See also James Laue's analogous account of Black Muslim prophecy, "A Contemporary Revitalization Movement in American Race Relations: The 'Black Muslims,' " *Social Forces* 42 (March 1964): 315–23.

8. Heidegger has repeated this story in many places. The following rendition is found in *The Question of Technology* For an excellent summary, see Zimmerman, *Heidegger's Confrontation with Modernity*, pp. 166–90.

9. Plato, *The Republic*, trans. G.M.A. Grube (Indianapolis, IN: Hackett Publishing Co., 1974), book VII, para. 514a–517b.

10. Zimmerman, *Heidegger's Confrontation with Modernity*, pp. 170–71, 176–78.

11. Max Weber, *Ancient Judaism*, trans. Hans Gerth and Don Martindale (Glencoe, IL: Free Press, 1951).

12. John Calvin, *On God and Man*, ed. F. W. Strothmann (New York: Frederick Ungar Publishing Co., 1966), p. 26.

13. Ecclesiasticus 9:9. "[Her] lips . . . are like a dripping honeycomb and her throat smoother than oil; but her end is as bitter as wormwood and her tongue is as sharp as a two-edged sword" (Proverbs 5:3–4). Cf. Lothario Dei Segni (Pope Innocent III), *On the Misery of the Human Condition*, trans. Donald R. Howard (New York: Bobbs-Merrill Co., 1969), pp. 48–50.

14. This is to say nothing of the Protestant's anxiety-driven need to certify their salvific status by making the world over after God's commandments. See Max Weber, *The Protestant Ethic and the Spirit of Capitalism*, trans. Talcott Parsons (New York: Charles Scribner's Sons, 1930).

15. Nietzsche, *The Will to Power*, pp. 463–64.

16. E. P. Thompson, "Notes on Exterminism, the Last Stage of Civilisation," in his *Beyond the Cold War* (New York: Pantheon Books, 1982), pp. 41–79. See also Edith Wyschogrod, *Spirit in Ashes: Hegel, Heidegger, and Man-Made Mass Death* (New Haven, CT: Yale University Press, 1985).

17. The idea of surrender-catch sociology is found in various writings of Kurt Wolff. See his "From Nothing to Sociology," *Philosophy of Social Science* 19 (1989): 321–39.

BIBLIOGRAPHY

Aho, James. *The Politics of Righteousness*. Seattle: University of Washington Press, 1990.

———. "The Recent Ethnogenesis of 'White Man.' " *Left Bank* 5 (1993): 55–64.

———. *Religious Mythology and the Art of War*. Westport, CT: Greenwood Press, 1981.

———. *This Thing of Darkness: A Sociology of the Enemy*. Seattle: University of Washington Press, 1994.

Alcoholics Anonymous. New York: Alcoholics Anonymous World Services, Inc., 1976 (1939).

Allen, Theodore. *The Invention of the White Race*. New York: Verso, 1994.

Apuleius. *Amor and Psyche: The Psychic Development of the Female*. Translated by Ralph Manheim with commentary by Erich Neumann. Princeton, NJ: Princeton University Press, 1956.

Asante, Molefi. *The Afrocentric Idea*. Philadelphia: Temple University Press, 1987.

Austin, John. *How To Do Things with Words*. New York: Oxford University Press, 1965.

Barber, Bernard. "Acculturation and Messianic Movements." *American Sociological Review* 6 (October 1941): 663–69.

Barkun, Michael. *Religion and the Racist Right: The Origins of the Christian Identity Movement*. Chapel Hill: University of North Carolina Press, 1994.

Barrett, William. *Irrational Man: A Study in Existential Philosophy*. Garden City, NY: Doubleday-Anchor, 1962.

Beauvoir, Simone de. *The Second Sex*. Translated by H. M. Parshley. New York: Vintage Books, 1949.

Becker, Ernest. *Angel in Armor*. New York: Free Press, 1969.

———. *The Denial of Death*. New York: Free Press, 1973.

———. *Escape from Evil*. New York: Free Press, 1975.

———. *The Structure of Evil*. New York: Free Press, 1968.

Bell, Susan. "Changing Ideas: The Medicalization of Menopause." In *The Meanings of Menopause*, edited by R. Rormanek. Hillsdale, NJ: Analytic Press, 1990.

Bellah, Robert, et al. *Habits of the Heart: Individualism and Commitment in American Life*. New York: Harper and Row, 1986.

Berger, Arthur A. *Signs in Contemporary Culture*. New York: Longman, 1984.

Berger, Peter, and Luckmann, Thomas. *The Social Construction of Reality*. Garden City, NY: Doubleday-Anchor, 1967.

Berlin, Brent. *Ethnobiological Classification*. Princeton, NJ: Princeton University Press, 1992.

Berman, Marshall. *All That Is Solid Melts into the Air*. New York: Simon and Schuster, 1982.

Bettelheim, Bruno. *Symbolic Wounds*. New York: Collier Books, 1954.

Blonsky, Marshall. *On Signs*. Baltimore, MD: Johns Hopkins University Press, 1985.

Bloom, Amy. "The Body Lies." *The New Yorker*, 18 July 1994.

Bloomfield, Morton. *The Seven Deadly Sins*. East Lansing: Michigan State University Press, 1952.

Bolinger, Dwight. *Aspects of Language*. New York: Harcourt, Brace and World, 1968.

Brown, Norman. *Life against Death*. Middletown, CT: Wesleyan University Press, 1973.

Buffon, Georges Louis Leclerc. *A Natural History of the Globe, of Man, . . .* New York: Leavitt & Allen, 1857 (1749).

Bunkers, Suzanne. *In Search of Susanna*. Iowa City: University of Iowa Press, 1996.

Calvin, John. *On God and Man*. Edited by F. W. Strothmann. New York: Frederick Ungar Publishing Co., 1966.

Campbell, Joseph. *The Masks of God*. 4 vol. New York: Viking Press, Inc., 1970.

Carmichael, Leonard. "The Early Growth of Language Capacity in the Individual." In *New Directions in the Study of Language*. Edited by Eric Lenneberg. Cambridge, MA: Massachusetts Institute of Technology, 1996.

Charmaz, Kathy. "Loss of Self: A Fundamental Form of Suffering in the Chronically Ill." *Sociology of Health and Illness* 5 (1983): 168–95.

Clifford, Michael. "Postmodern Thought and the End of Man." In *The Question of the Other*, edited by Arleen Dallery and Charles Scott. Albany: State University of New York Press, 1989.

Conrad, Peter. "The Experience of Illness: Recent and New Directions." *Research in the Sociology of Health Care* 6 (1987): 1–31.

Cooley, Charles Horton. *Human Nature and Social Order*. New York: Charles Scribner's Sons, 1902.

Coulter, Jeff. *The Social Construction of Mind: Studies in Ethnomethodology and Linguistic Philosophy*. Totowa, NJ: Rowan and Littlefield, 1979.

Curtiss, Susan. *Genie: A Psycholinguistic Study of a Modern Day "Wild-Child."* New York: Academic Press, 1977.

Denzinger, Heinrich. *The Sources of Catholic Dogma*. Translated by Roy Deferari. St. Louis, MO: Herder Book Co., 1957.

Derrida, Jacques. *Writing and Difference*. Translated and introduced by Alan Bass. Chicago: University of Chicago Press, 1978.

Dollard, John, et al. *Frustration and Aggression*. New Haven, CT: Yale University Press, 1939.

Durkheim, Emile. *The Division of Labor in Society*. Translated by George Simpson. New York: Free Press, 1964 (1893).

———. *The Elementary Forms of Religious Life*. Translated by Joseph Ward Swain. Glencoe, IL: Free Press, 1969.

Eliade, Mircea. *Rites and Symbols of Initiation*. New York: Harper and Row, 1958.

Ellen, Roy and Reason, David, eds. *Classifications in their Social Context*. New York: Academic Press, 1979.

Erchak, Gerald, and Rosenfeld, Richard. "Learning Disabilities, Dyslexia, and the Medicalization of the Classroom." In *Images of Issues*, edited by Joel Best. Hawthorne, NY: Aldine de Gruyter

Erenreich, Barbara, and English, Deirdre. *Complaints and Disorders: The Sexual Politics of Sickness*. Old Westbury, NY: Feminist Press, 1973.

Fay, Brian. *Contemporary Philosophy of Social Science*. Cambridge, MA: Blackwell, 1996.

Figert, Anne E. *Women and the Ownership of PMS: The Structuring of a Psychiatric Disorder*. Hawthorne, NY: Aldine de Gruyter, 1996.

Foucault, Michel. *The History of Sexuality*. 3 vols. Translated by Robert Hurley. New York: Pantheon, 1978.

———. *Madness and Civilization*. Translated by Richard Howard. New York: Random House, 1965.

Frazer, James G. *The Golden Bough*. New York: Macmillan, 1951 (1921).

Freund, Peter, and McGuire, Meredith. *Health, Illness and the Social Body.* 2d ed. Englewood Cliffs, NJ: Prentice-Hall, 1995.

Frisch, Karl von. *The Dancing Bees.* Translated by Dora Ilse. London: Reader's Union/Methuen, 1955.

Fromm, Erich. *Marx's Concept of Man.* New York: Ungar, 1961.

Fuller, Robert. *Naming the Antichrist.* New York: Oxford University Press, 1995.

Gans, Herbert. *Urban Villagers.* New York: Free Press, 1962.

Garfinkel, Harold. "Conditions of Successful Degradation Ceremonies." *American Journal of Sociology* 61 (1956): 420–24.

———. *Studies in Ethnomethodology.* Englewood Cliffs, NJ: Prentice-Hall, 1967.

Gates, Henry Louis, Jr. "Race as the Trope of the World." In *Race, Writing and Difference,* edited by Henry Louis Gates, Jr. Chicago: University of Chicago Press, 1986.

Girard, Rene. *Violence and the Sacred.* Translated by Patrick Gregory. Baltimore, MD: Johns Hopkins University Press, 1977.

Goffman, Erving. *Asylums.* Chicago: Aldine Publishing Co., 1962.

———. *Interaction Ritual.* Garden City, NY: Doubleday-Anchor, 1967.

———. *The Presentation of Self in Everyday Life.* Garden City, NY: Doubleday-Anchor, 1959.

Goode, Erich, and Ben-Yehuda, Nachman. *Moral Panics: The Social Construction of Deviance.* Cambridge, MA: Blackwell, 1994.

Gusfield, Joseph. *Community: A Critical Response.* New York: Harper and Row, 1975.

Haines, John. *The Stars, the Snow, the Fire.* St. Paul, MN: Greywolf, 1989.

Hamsun, Knut. *Growth of the Soil.* Translated by W. W. Worster. New York: Vintage Books, 1972 (1921).

Haring, Bernard. "The Phenomenology of the Scrupulous Conscience." In *The Law of Christ.* Edited by Bernard Haring. Cork, Ireland: Mercier Press, 1963.

Harris, G. Christian, M.D. "Abusing the Abuser—I'm Only Trying to Help You." Paper presented at the Seventh Annual Symposium of the American College of Forensic Psychiatry. San Diego, CA: 31 March 1989.

Harris, Thomas. *I'm OK, You're OK.* New York: Harper and Row,1969.

Haugen, Einar. "Linguistic Relativity: Myths and Methods." In *Language and Thought: Anthropological Issues,* edited by W. C. McCormack and S. A. Wurm. The Hague: Mouton, 1977.

Heidegger, Martin. *Being and Time.* Translated by John Macquarri and Edward Robinson. New York: Harper and Row, 1962.

————. *The Question of Technology and Other Essays*. Translated and introduced by William Lovitt. New York: Harper and Row, 1977.

Hewitt, John. *The Myth of Self-Esteem*. New York: St. Martin's Press, 1998.

————. *Self & Society*. 5th ed. Boston: Allyn and Bacon, 1991.

Hewitt, John, and Stokes, Randall. "Disclaimers." *American Sociological Review* 40 (February 1975): 1–11.

Hobsbawm, Eric, and Ranger, Terence. *The Invention of Tradition*. Cambridge, UK: Cambridge University Press, 1983.

Hochschild, Arlie. *The Managed Heart: The Commercialization of Emotion*. Berkeley: University of California Press, 1983.

Holstein, James, and Miller, Gale. "Social Constructionism and Social Problems Work." In *Constructionist Controversies*, edited by James Holstein and Gale Miller. New York: Aldine de Gruyter, 1993.

Hughes, Everett C. "Good People and Dirty Work." In *The Sociological Eye: Selected Papers*. New York: Aldine and Atherton, 1971.

Huizinga, Johann. *Homo Ludens*. Translated by R.F.C. Hull. London: Routledge & Kegan Paul. 1949.

Husserl, Edmund. *Cartesian Meditations: An Introduction to Phenomenology*. Translated by Dorian Cairns. The Hague: Martinus Nijhoff, 1977.

————. "Philosophy and the Crisis of European Man." In his *Phenomenology and the Crisis of Philosophy*. New York: Harper and Row, 1965.

Ignatiev, Noel. *How the Irish Became "White."* New York: Routledge, 1994.

Illich, Ivan. *Medical Nemesis: The Expropriation of Health*. New York: Pantheon, 1976.

Jehenson, Roger. "A Phenomenological Approach to the Study of the Formal Organization." In *Phenomenological Sociology*, edited by George Psathas. New York: John Wiley & Sons, 1973.

Jung, Carl. *The Undiscovered Self*. Translated by R.F.C. Hull. New York: Mentor Books, 1957.

Katz, Jonathan. "The Age of Sodomitical Sin, 1607–1740." In *Reclaiming Sodom*, edited by Jonathan Goldberg. New York: Routledge, 1994.

————. *The Invention of Heterosexuality*. New York: Penguin Books, 1995.

Keen, Sam. *Faces of the Enemy: Reflections of the Hostile Imagination*. San Francisco: Harper and Row, 1986.

Kierkegaard, Søren. "The Present Age." Translated by Alexander Dru. In *A Kierkegaard Anthology*, edited by Robert Bretall. New York: The Modern Library, 1946.

King, Hunt. "Inventing the Indian: White Images, Oral Literature, and Contemporary Native Writers." Ph.D. diss., University of Utah, 1986.

Kitzinger, Celia. *The Social Construction of Lesbianism*. Newbury Park, CA: Sage 1987.

Kleinman, Arthur. *The Illness Narratives: Suffering, Healing and the Human Condition*. New York: Basic Books, 1988.

Klineberg, Otto. *Social Psychology*. Rev. ed. New York: Holt, Rinehart & Winston, 1954.

Krafft-Ebing, Richard. *Psychopathia Sexualis: With Especial Reference to the Anti-Pathic Instinct*. Brooklyn, NY: Physicians and Surgeons Books, 1922 (1892).

Kuhn, Thomas. *The Structure of Scientific Revolutions*. 2d ed. enl. Chicago: University of Chicago Press, 1970.

Laue, James. "A Contemporary Revitalization Movement in American Race Relations: The 'Black Muslims.' " *Social Forces* 42 (March 1964): 315–23.

Leese, Arnold. *Jewish Ritual Murder*. London: International Fascist League, 1938.

Lemert, Charles. "Dark Thoughts about the Self." In *Social Theory and the Politics of Identity*, edited by Craig Calhoun. Cambridge, MA: Blackwell, 1994.

Levinas, Emmanuel. *Otherwise Than Being*. Translated by Alphonso Lingus. The Hague: Martinus Nijhoff, 1981.

Lindesmith, Alfred; Strauss, Anselm; and Denzin, Norman. *Social Psychology*. 6th ed. Englewood Cliffs, NJ: Prentice-Hall, 1988.

Loftus, Elizabeth. *Witness for the Defense*. New York: St. Martin's Press, 1991.

Lothario Dei Segni (Pope Innocent III). *On the Misery of the Human Condition*. Translated by Donald R. Howard. New York: Bobbs-Merrill Co., 1969.

Maddock, Kenneth. *The Australian Aborigines*. Harmondsworth, UK: Penguin, 1974.

Maitz, E. A., and Pekala, R. J. "Phenomenological Quantification of an Out-of-Body Experience Associated with a Near-Death Event." *Omega* 22 (1990/91): 199–214.

Marcuse, Herbert. *Eros and Civilization*. Boston: Beacon Press, 1955.

———. *One-Dimensional Man*. Boston: Beacon Press, 1964.

Marx, Karl, and Engels, Friedrich. *The Communist Manifesto*. New York: International Publishers, 1930 (1848).

McNeill, John T. "Medicine for Sin as Prescribed in the Penitentials." *Church History* 1 (1932): 14–26.

McNeill, John T., and Gamer, Helena M., trans., ed., and intro. *Medieval Handbooks of Penance*. New York: Columbia University Press, 1938.

McNeill, William. *The Rise of the West*. Chicago: University of Chicago Press, 1963.

Mead, George Herbert. *Mind, Self and Society*. Edited by Charles W. Morris. Chicago: University of Chicago Press, 1934.

Mehan, Hugh, and Wood, Houston. *The Reality of Ethnomethodology*. New York: John Wiley and Sons, 1977.

Menninger, Karl. *Whatever Became of Sin?* New York: Hawthorn Books, 1973.

Merleau-Ponty, Maurice. "On the Phenomenology of Language." In *Phenomenology, Language and Sociology*, edited by John O'Neill. London: Heinemann, 1974

———. *Phenomenology of Perception*. Translated by C. Smith. Atlantic Highlands, NJ: Humanities Press, 1962.

Mills, C. Wright. "Situated Actions and the Vocabulary of Motives." *American Sociological Review* 5 (December 1940): 904–13.

Mills, C. Wright, and Gerth, Hans. *Character and Social Structure*. New York: Harcourt, Brace and World, 1953.

Morgan, Murray. *The Last Wilderness*. Seattle: University of Washington Press, 1955.

Morishima, Michio. *Why Has Japan "Succeeded?" Western Technology and the Japanese Ethos*. London: Cambridge University Press, 1982.

Morris, David. *The Culture of Pain*. Berkeley: University of California Press, 1991.

Myrdal, Gunnar. *The American Dilemma*. New York: Harper and Brothers, 1944.

Myss, Caroline. *The Anatomy of the Spirit*. New York: Three Rivers Press, 1996.

Neils-Conzen, Kathleen. "German Americans and the Invention of Ethnicity." In *Germans in America*, edited by Randall Miller. Philadelphia: German Society of America, 1984.

Neumann, Erich. *The Origins and History of Consciousness*. Princeton, NJ: Princeton University Press, 1973 (1954).

Nietzsche, Friedrich. "The Gay Science." In *The Portable Nietzsche*, translated and edited by Walter Kaufmann. New York: Vintage Books, 1954.

————. *The Will to Power*. Translated by Walter Kaufmann and R. J. Hollingdale. New York: Vintage Books, 1968.

Nimmons, David. "Sex and the Brain." *Discover*, March 1994, pp. 64–71.

Novak, Michael. *The Rise of the Unmeltable Ethnics*. New York: Macmillan, 1975.

Ostrow, James. *Social Sensitivity*. Albany: State University of New York Press, 1990.

————. "Spontaneous Involvement and Social Life." *Sociological Perspectives* 39 (Fall 1996): 341–51.

Ovid. *Ovid: The Metamorphoses*. Translated by Horace Gregory. New York: Viking Press, 1958.

Parsons, Talcott. *The Social System*. New York: Free Press, 1951.

Paz, Octavio. *The Labyrinth of Solitude: Life and Thought in Mexico*. Translated by Lysander Kemp. New York: Grove Press, 1961.

Pfohl, Stephen. "The Discovery of Child Abuse." *Social Problems* 24 (1977): 310–23.

Phillips, Katherine. *The Broken Mirror*. New York: Oxford University Press, 1996.

Pieper, Josef. *About Love*. Translated by Richard Winston and Clara Winston. Chicago: Franciscan Herald Press, 1974.

————. *The Four Cardinal Virtues*. Notre Dame, IN: Notre Dame University Press, 1966.

Plank, Richard. *The Pink Triangle: The Nazi War against Homosexuals*. New York: Henry Holt, 1986.

Plato, "Phaedo." In *Great Dialogues of Plato*, translated by W.H.D. Rouse. New York: Mentor Books, 1956.

————. *Philebus & Epinomis*. Translated by A. E. Taylor. London: Dawsons and Pall Mall, 1972.

————. *The Republic*. Translated by G.M.A. Grube. Indianapolis, IN: Hackett Publishing Co., 1974.

————. "Symposium." In *The Dialogues of Plato*. Translated by B. Jowett. New York: Random House, 1937.

Poliakov, Leon. *The Aryan Myth*. New York: Basic Books, 1971.

Prepare War. Pontiac, MO: Covenant, Sword and the Arm of the Lord Bookstore, n.d.

Protocols of the Learned Elders of Zion. Translated by Victor Marsden. N.p. 1905.

Rand, Ayn. *The Virtue of Selfishness: A New Concept of Egoism*. New York: Times-Mirror, 1961.

Reinarman, Craig, and Levine, Harry G. "The Crack Attack: Politics and

Media in America's Latest Drug Scare." In *Images of Issues*, edited by Joel Best. Hawthorne, NY: Aldine de Gruyter, 1989.

Reisman, Leonard. *The Lonely Crowd*. New Haven, CT: Yale University Press, 1953.

Rich, Adrienne. "Compulsory Heterosexuality and Lesbian Existence." In *Powers of Desire*, edited by A. Sitnow, C. Stanwell, and S. Thompson. New York: Monthly Review Press, 1983.

Roheim, Geza. *The Riddle of the Sphinx*. New York: Harper and Row, 1974 (1934).

Romanyshyn, Robert, and Whalen, Brian. "Depression and the American Dream: The Struggle with Home." In *Pathologies of the Modern Self*, edited by David Michael Levin. New York: New York University Press, 1987.

Ross, Edward A. *The Old World and the New*. New York: Century, 1914.

Said, Edward. *Orientalism*. New York: Vintage Books, 1978.

Sanders, William. "Rape Investigations." In *Sociology of Deviance*, edited by Jack Douglas. Boston: Allyn and Bacon, 1984.

Saussure, Ferdinand de. *Course in General Semantics*. Translated by Wade Baskin, edited by Charles Baly and Albert Sechehaye. New York: Harper-Collins, 1965.

Schacter, Stanley, and Singer, David. "Cognitive, Social and Physiological Determinants of Emotional State." *Psychological Review* 69 (1962): 379–99.

Scheler, Max. *The Nature of Sympathy*. Translated by Peter Heath, introduced by Werner Stark. London: Routledge & Kegan Paul, 1958.

————. *On Feeling, Knowing, and Valuing*. Edited and introduced by Harold J. Bershady. Chicago: University of Chicago Press, 1992.

Scherer, Klaus. "Relating Situation Evaluation to Emotion Differentiation." In *Facets of Emotion: Recent Research*, edited by Klaus Scherer. Hillsdale, NJ: Lawrence Erlbaum Associates, 1988.

Schott, Robin May. *Cognition and Eros: A Critique of the Kantian Paradigm*. Boston: Beacon Press, 1988.

Schutz, Alfred. *Collected Papers*. 3 vols. Edited and introduced by Maurice Natanson. The Hague: Martinus Nijhoff, 1973.

Schutz, Alfred, and Luckmann, Thomas. *The Structures of the Life-World*. Translated by Richard Zaner and H. Tristam Engelhardt, Jr. Evanston, IL: Northwestern University Press, 1973.

Scott, Marvin, and Lyman, Stanford. "Accounts." *American Sociological Review* 33 (December 1968): 46–62.

Searle, John. *The Construction of Social Reality*. New York: Free Press, 1975.

Seward, Jack. *Hara-Kiri: Japanese Ritual Suicide*. Rutland, VT: Charles E. Tuttle Co., 1968.

Silverman, Katja. *The Subject of Semiotics*. New York: Oxford University Press, 1983.

Simmel, Georg. *Conflict and the Web of Group Affiliations*. Translated by Kurt Wolff and Reinhard Bendix. Glencoe, IL: Free Press, 1955.

———. *The Problems of the Philosophy of History: An Epistemological Essay*. Translated by Guy Oakes. New York: Free Press, 1977.

———. "Sociability." In *The Sociology of Georg Simmel*, translated and edited by Kurt H. Wolff. New York: Free Press, 1964.

Solomon, Jack. *The Signs of Our Times*. New York: Harper and Row, 1988.

Spelman, Elisabeth. *Inessential Woman*. Boston: Beacon Press, 1989.

Spiegelberg, Herbert. "On the Right to Say 'We': A Linguistic and Phenomenological Analysis." In *Phenomenological Sociology*, edited by George Psathas. New York: John Wiley & Sons, 1973.

Starr, Paul. *The Transformation of American Medicine*. New York: Basic Books, 1982.

Stein, Edith. *On the Nature of Empathy*. Translated by Waltraut Stein. The Hague: Martinus Nijhoff, 1964.

Stein, Maurice. *The Eclipse of Community*. New York: Harper and Row, 1964.

Stevenson, I., and Greyson, B. "The Phenomenology of Near-Death Experiences," *American Journal of Psychiatry* 137 (1980): 1193–95.

Strauss, Anselm. *Negotiation: Varieties, Contexts, Processes and Social Order*. San Francisco: Jossey-Bass, 1978.

Sykes, Charles. *Nation of Victims: The Decay of American Character*. New York: St. Martin's Press, 1992.

Sykes, Gresham. "Techniques of Neutralization, a Theory of Delinquency." *American Sociological Review* 22 (December 1957): 664–70.

Szasz, Thomas. *Ceremonial Chemistry*. Garden City, NY: Doubleday-Anchor, 1975.

———. *The Manufacture of Madness*. New York: Dell Publishing Co., Inc., 1970.

Talbot, Margaret. "Dial-a-Wife." *New Yorker*, 20 & 27 October 1997, 196–208.

Tentler, Thomas N. *Sin and Confession on the Eve of the Reformation*. Princeton, NJ: Princeton University Press, 1977.

Thompson, E. P. *Beyond the Cold War*. New York: Pantheon Books, 1982.

Toennies, Ferdinand. *Community and Society*. Translated by Charles Loomis. East Lansing: Michigan State University Press, 1957.

Treitschke, Heinrich von. *Politics*. Translated by Blanche Dugdale and Torben de Bille. New York: Harcourt, Brace and World, 1963.

Turner, Ralph H. "Role-Taking, Role-Standpoint, and Reference Group Behavior." *American Journal of Sociology* 61 (1956): 316–28.

Vaughan, Alden. "From White Man to Redskin: Changing Anglo-American Perceptions of the American Indian." *American Historical Journal* 87 (October 1982): 917–53.

Voegelin, Eric. *Israel and Revelation*. Baton Rouge: Louisiana State University Press, 1956.

Wallace, Anthony. "Revitalization Movements." *American Anthropologist* 58 (1956): 264–81.

Weber, Max. *Ancient Judaism*. Translated by Hans Gerth and Don Martindale. Glencoe, IL: Free Press, 1951.

———. *The Protestant Ethic and the Spirit of Capitalism*. Translated by Talcott Parsons. New York: Charles Scribner's Sons, 1930.

———. *The Religion of China: Confucianism and Taoism*. Translated by Hans Gerth. New York: Macmillan, 1951.

———. *The Theory of Social and Economic Organization*. Translated and introduced by Talcott Parsons. New York: Free Press, 1947.

Weeks, Jeffrey. "Sexual Identification Is a Strange Thing." *Against Nature: Essays on History, Sexuality and Identity*. London: Rivers Oram Press, 1991.

Weitz, Rose. "Uncertainty and the Lives of Persons with AIDS." In *The Sociology of Health & Illness*, edited by Peter Conrad and Rochelle Kern. 4th ed. New York: St. Martin's Press, 1994.

Whorf, Benjamin. *Language, Thought and Reality*. Edited and introduced by John Carroll. Cambridge, MA: Massachusetts Institute of Technology, 1956.

Whyte, William H. *The Organization Man*. Garden City, NY: Doubleday-Anchor, 1957.

Wolfe, Thomas. *Radical Chic & Mau-Mauing the Flak-Catchers*. New York: Farrar, Straus and Giroux, 1970.

Wolff, Kurt. "From Nothing to Sociology." *Philosophy of Social Science* 19 (1989): 321–39.

Wright, Lawrence. *Remembering Satan*. New York: Alfred A. Knopf, 1994.

Wyschogrod, Edith. *Spirit in Ashes: Hegel, Heidegger, and Man-Made Mass Death*. New Haven, CT: Yale University Press, 1985.

Xenophon. *Memoriabilia*. Translated by J. W. Watson. New York: E. P. Dutton, 1927.

Zimmerman, Michael. *Heidegger's Confrontation with Modernity*. Bloomington: Indiana University Press, 1990.

INDEX

About the Author

JAMES A. AHO is Professor of Sociology at Idaho State University in Pocatello, where he has taught since 1969. He is the author of five books, including *Religious Mythology and the Art of War* (Greenwood, 1981) and *This Thing of Darkness: A Sociology of the Enemy* (1994).

ISBN 0-275-96247-4